The BODY OF CHRIST

The
BODY OF CHRIST
Jean-Jacques Trifault

Footsteps to Wisdom Publishing

The Body of Christ by Jean-Jacques Trifault
Copyright © 2010 by Jean-Jacques Trifault

Editors: Diane Fernsler, Mary Trifault, Sharon Valin
Book cover and interior design: Kasia Krawczyk

All rights reserved.
No part of this book may be reproduced in any form or by any electronic or mechanical means, including information storage and retrieval systems, without permission in writing from the author, except by a reviewer who may quote brief passages in a review.

First American Edition

Published by Footsteps To Wisdom Publishing
For questions and comments visit
www.footstepstowisdom.org

ISBN-13 978-0-9797877-6-8
ISBN-10 0-9797877-6-9

Table of Contents

Introduction   11

Are We Promoting a Divine Purpose or a Destructive Purpose?   15

Choose Wisely Your Idol   73

The Philosophy of We or I   123

Symbols of God's Love   181

Introduction

"The Body of Christ" contains four speeches that reflect upon the life of Christ while in his physical body on Earth. How did Christ develop his divinity, and what relationship can we hope to have with him? These speeches explore the ability and responsibility of human beings to direct our destinies in relationship to God and to the Christ, through our choice of perceptions.

In the first speech, "Choose Wisely Your Idol", the author examines the connection between thought and feeling as they relate to spiritual growth. For those of us who are accustomed to feeling a lot of emotion and not questioning where it comes from, this description may come as a surprise, even as radical, in its insightful presentation. The author explains the role that worship plays in developing our attitudes, emotions and behavior, and shows how Jesus himself, through worshipping his Heavenly Father, could receive the love he needed to grow to divine perfection.

"Do We Carry a Divine or a Destructive Purpose?" examines why, even though we all desire for goodness, humans still produce a never-ending history of conflict. Could we have two purposes 'programmed' within us, one promoting duality and harmony and the other promoting opposition and selfishness? The author explains how living according to the laws of duality, as Jesus did, will enable us to remove our destructive 'program' and allow God's love to dwell in us as it dwells in Christ.

In "The Philosophy of We or I", the author examines our universal desire to transform ourselves and our society for the better, and the disillusionment that many people experience as they study various philosophies. A philosophy may appear inspirational and sophisticated but in reality promotes selfishness or centering on the 'I'. The author introduces Jesus Christ as a 'doctor of divine philosophy' who promotes a philosophy of 'We' through his words and parables, showing how following God's laws of duality will allow us to experience the love of God and to create the Kingdom of Heaven on Earth.

"The Symbols of God's Love" explores the tenacity and faith required to make a transformation, whether it be a scientific or medical 'breakthrough', or a deeper relationship with the invisible God. Religions have traditionally used certain symbols to help strengthen their faith in God, and Jesus himself presented his disciples with two famous symbols, the bread and the wine, as physical reminders of his love for humankind. Since physical symbols can help us in our quest to discover the invisible love of God, can we therefore expand our quantity of symbols? Christ walked through the countryside, with its hills, streams, flora and fauna, villages and towns, and brought holiness to these places through his presence; therefore, all these kinds of places and things can be viewed as symbols or reminders of Christ's love. His parables reflect his deep love for his environment and for his people, and remind us of to view all people and all things as holy in order to allow us to receive the full love of God.

We are now invited to take the journey to discover the divine mind of Christ that created his pure, divine body. Christ shed his sweat and tears and blood in order to gain his divinity, rather than just being born into perfection, and the holy path he led enables him to exhort us to also invest our utmost to become "perfect as our Heavenly Father is perfect" by following the example of Christ's life.

Are We Promoting a Divine Purpose or a Destructive Purpose?

The question we want to ask ourselves today is, "Do we know the original purpose of our own existence?"

One way to determine our purpose is to observe the dynamics within our minds. What we will find is that there are two major aspects, or parts, of our minds. One part perceives the more dominant and visible aspects of what is around us and we could refer to it as the subjective side, while the other part perceives the more intangible and invisible aspects and we could call it the objective side. These two parts allow us to see in two dimensions, as for example, vertically and horizontally, front and back, or inside and outside. These two parts are also reflected in our thinking, as for example, one group of our thoughts is more connected to the origin of our lives, to our background and our ancestors, while the other group of thoughts makes us look to our future, or one group of thoughts focuses more on our internal aspect and the other on physical appearance. In order for us to become united beings who can fulfill our purpose, we need to always use both sides of our being, the subjective side and the objective side.

Let us demonstrate this concept through a simple example. If we choose to apply only one color, like the color black, to create a painting, surely the black alone will be difficult to enjoy until we add a second color, like the color white. If we paint with both black and white, we can create an image that is much more pleasant than if we just use black alone. Similarly, if we only choose the color white, regardless how great that color can be, we know that it cannot create a perceivable shape until we use some lines of black, or of some other color, especially if we would like to create some design. When a black line is added to a white background, the color white begins to have purpose as well as the color black becomes valuable, and both colors together create pleasure when we look at them.

Let us take another example. As we know, when the sun rises the darkness and the light are in their transition period, in other words, the darkness diminishes and the light becomes amplified. At a specific moment of the sunrise, at the time when these aspects are in balance and as we see a spectrum of colors, we regard this event as the most beautiful time of the sunrise. As well, at the end of the day when the sun is setting, we also consider this period, when light fades and the dusk sets in, as a beautiful moment. On a broader scale, regardless we enjoy seeing the night coming after a day of sunlight, we are also happy again when we see the brightness coming out of that deep night, the light that during the night is only reflected by the moon.

In these events of the night changing into the day and vice versa we can observe that in a specific moment one pole is more subjective or more perceivable while the other pole is more objective or less perceivable. As well, depending on the time of the day, each pole can switch its role, with one pole increasing or taking the position of subject while the other pole decreases or takes the position of object. If the night wants to increase, the sun has to decrease and if the sun wants to increase, the night has to decrease. We can say that when the sun rises, its light is dominant. But when the evening comes, we can see the night, which was dormant all day, becoming subject. In this sense, when one pole becomes stronger, the other becomes weaker; yet we consider the most beautiful moment to be when both poles are in balance with each other.

The same is true when we look at a painting or a drawing. We consider a painting is beautiful when the aspects of the subjective colors that are more active and the aspects of the objective colors that are more passive are in harmony with each other. From these examples we can conclude that beauty is created through the combination of colors and the duality between them, whether this combination was consciously created by a human being or it already existed within the creation.

After realizing that beauty is created through the composition of two major poles that are in relationship, or duality, with each other, let us take a look at human beings. We can say if our mind operates based on this concept of duality, then whatever we will think and do will be based on creating or maintaining duality, or relationship. When we have achieved this, we will always be viewed as being beautiful or, as fulfilling our purpose. Vice versa, if human beings do not think and act based on duality and instead think and act based on lack of duality, they will be unable to create beauty or fulfill their purpose. In other words, if we have a tendency to always take opposition to another pole, we will have immense difficulty to create harmony and the result will not have the same appearance as the result of the one who harmonizes with other poles.

The Harmony Within Our Mind

When we look at the world today, we realize it is complex, confused and many times violent. From this we can assume that human beings do not operate harmoniously, or to look at it in another way, they do not have a 'directive' within themselves that encourages them to think and act based on duality. To have created this world of complaint and opposition they must be operating on another directive, or 'program', which prevents them from perceiving duality and from acting based on duality. Consequently, realizing their purpose, and achieving beauty and divinity, is still an issue for all humanity. And at times just hearing words like 'beauty', 'goodness' or 'divinity' causes some rejection within people, perhaps because they believe these words exist only in fairy tales.

What is the reason that human beings can have this attitude toward words that describe such a worthy purpose? It can only be that they must carry a 'program' inside the blueprint of their minds that does not direct them to achieve beauty and divinity. Then how do we discern the program we carry? As we know, usually human beings think before they act. Since every thought originates from what is printed inside our brains, we can understand the program inside our blueprint by examining the way our thoughts are built. Besides digging within our thoughts, we can also understand the program we are following by observing the patterns of our behavior.

Once we realize the program inside our brain is not based on creating duality but based on opposing duality, and with this understanding look at the world of today and perceive all the chaos that is around us, we can conclude that our world actually is an extension of what is inside of us. We will see indeed we are programmed to follow a destructive purpose, which is reflected in our thoughts and actions. Nevertheless, once we are aware of what has happened to us and we decide to instead adopt a program that leads us to promote the qualities of harmony and creativity, allowing us to fulfill a divine purpose, we can transform all our thoughts in a positive manner, which sooner or later will also influence our physical actions.

Based on this understanding we truly might wish to reprogram our destructive blueprint, or what could also be described as our destructive 'microchip', in the hope of building a microchip that carries only aspects of duality, so that we can fulfill our purpose or destiny of becoming beautiful and divine. In actuality, to reconstruct thoughts of duality within our minds, we have to re-educate ourselves based on the viewpoint of duality over a period of time. In doing so we will be able re-print in ourselves the original design that, like every other creation, we were meant to carry since the beginning of our existence.

As just explained, we can perceive what is printed in our 'microchip' based on the way we think and act. Do we see ourselves creating harmony and peace or do we see ourselves creating rejection and opposition? The moment we start to see ourselves opposing whatever presents itself to us, it means we are trying to promote one side or one 'pole' at the expense of the other 'pole'. By rejecting the other pole, we are trying to weaken it to the point of eliminating its existence. Therefore, if we see in ourselves the nature of always wanting to be dominant and refusing to be accomodating, it would be wise to remind ourselves of the sun. If the sun were to continue to shine on the land for twenty-four hours each day, then the land would become dry. In the same manner, if the night wanted to dominate, it would be immensely difficult for any plants to live. Similarly, if we always think and act as subjects in relation to everything around us, we surely will create characters so powerful that people will have a hard time to live around us. They will be fearful of us, like the plants would become fearful of the sun or of the night without the sun, if either of these two poles were to persist in maintaining their subjective position twenty-four hours long.

If we apply this situation to the color spectrum, it would mean that one color, for example, blue, becomes totally dominant, to the point that any other color would have no place to exist. Surely, if our colorful world suddenly transformed into only one color, this event would have an effect on all of us. Maybe the aspect of duality and harmony between subject and object does not appear so important for our physical survival, but if we want to create beauty, we need to realize the importance and power of each pole and consider its role according to the time and the place.

We might ask what force would allow a person to maintain the position of subject to everything around him or her for so many hours or days? Surely, in order to keep this attitude, this person must carry a strong feeling within him or herself in order to attain the energy to achieve that. This energy makes it difficult for this person to take the position of an objective pole. If we more closely examine the nature of this energy, we will realize it is an oppressive energy. This energy not only represses the objective character within the person who insists on his position of subjectivity, but at the same time it emits a feeling of oppression to the other poles who are living around him, so that they cannot develop themselves but instead become muted or dormant. An example of this might be the heat of the sun constantly warming the Earth, making the plants, which are in an objective position to the heat, shrivel or in some other way adapt themselves, as for example, the cactus have learned to do.

So if we have a tendency to always take the position of subject towards others, we become like a sun that is burning the ground. With this kind of character, if we present any of our thoughts to others, we promote them as the only ideas that are right. As well, we imply that whatever we do is the only right thing to do. In this kind of situation, people who are in the position of object to us feel quite overwhelmed by the power we display, to the point that they cannot even reveal to us the effect we have on them and they just can endure our presence. The strong emotions we create completely suppress them, even though we ourselves who take the subjective pole to them might not believe or perceive that we are the cause of their dilemma. Similarly, when the sun's heat is continuously projected on the land to its fullest degree, the plants will either begin to suffocate and die or to look for ways to restrain themselves in order to be able to survive. Even if the plants were able to speak to the sun, it is questionable if the sun would understand their situation, because it might believe that it is giving the maximum of its heat for the sake of nourishing the plants, knowing that without light there can be no life.

In a similar manner, the people who are around a person who maintains a subjective position throughout the day will always have to take an objective position if they are obliged to stay with this person and yet want to survive. In the process they will create characters within themselves that have many dormant aspects, like plants that are living in a desert under the scorching heat of the sun. And if these persons venture outside the territory where they were forced to remain in the position of objects, they will continue to display the nature of objects. Therefore, if we find someone who instinctively seeks the position of object, we can deduce he must have been around a person who always took the position of subject toward him. We can observe the same phenomenon of adaptation in animals. When one animal chooses to take a dominant position over a specific area, many animals that have been living there will either flee from that place in order to survive, or those who choose to stay will transform themselves to take a position of object in order to sustain their existence.

Imbalance Between Subjectivity and Objectivity

Observing these situations we might question why human beings display so much subjectivity when we can see this characteristic so highly diminishes the quality of life, to the point of destroying it. To give an answer, we indeed can only presume there must be a program inside our 'microchip' that directs us to want to maintain a subjective mind, which in turn demands us to perform subjective actions for many hours, days and months, if not years, without ordering us to switch our attitude and take a position that is more objective or receiving. Based on this observation, we can believe there must have been something that was introduced inside of us that continuously obliges us to focus on dominating others and refusing to surrender to anybody. Eventually we might realize that this program has been damaging and twisting our original program, which is also within us directing us to fulfill our divine purpose during the time we are living on this Earth.

Surely, if this is what happened to humankind, it is understandable why throughout history there was always one group of people who took the position of subject and dominated another group, forcing them to take the position of object. As long as nobody removed the dominating group from their position of subject and this group succeeded in maintaining their place for a prolonged period of time, it meant that the other groups around them somehow tolerated the position of the objective pole for that period of time. But once, for whatever reason, those in the subject position began to lose their power, the masses who had been in the objective position started to revolt against them. And even more than that, they felt now it was time for them to take over the group that had been dominating them and place themselves in the position of subject.

Regardless of how humankind acquired these domineering characteristics, surely the program inside our 'microchip' does not seem to value the position of object equally to the position of subject; instead, it sees them as being in opposition to each other. And by not recognizing these two poles as equally important, we cannot co-exist in a peaceful way. Even more, we cannot create something beautiful together, and instead we produce constant conflict.

We can perceive this phenomenon in our every day lives. Because we are unable or unwilling to take different positions according to each situation, we find ourselves in all kinds of discord with those around us. For example, we might ask someone a simple question, like "What did you do today?" and this person responds aggressively. This means, instead of taking the position of object when being asked this question, he chose to behave according to his subjective character and for this reason he became so unfriendly and defensive. If we ask the same question to someone who chooses silence as a response, this means he cannot take the position of subject after listening to our question, and retreats to an even more objective position, recoiling within himself to the point of removing himself from the relationship.

Most of the time these kinds of interactions in which one person becomes dominant or someone takes an oppressed position occur at high speed. For this reason we tend not to be aware of the effect of our behavior on the other person as well as on ourself. If we ask the person who usually takes a highly subjective position, "Why are you so domineering?" he might say, "I don't know what you are talking about. I was just expressing myself." And if we ask the one who tends to be unresponsive, "Why are you always quiet? Why don't you respond or say even just a few words?" he might answer, "I don't know. This is just the way I am."

Is this what we are meant to be? If so, we can say that we are pre-determined to always take the same position and we only take a different position when there is somebody more powerful than us forcing us to take that position. Surely, if we want to continue the past history of fear and misery, we will continue to choose this road of being the almighty subject or the powerless object.

However, if we seek for our original purpose, we will realize it asks us to take another road. It wants us to value each pole equally, the objective pole as well as the subjective pole. For this reason, when someone takes the position of subject toward another person and wants to fulfill this position in accordance with the original purpose of human beings, he has to first mature both the subjective part as well as the objective part of his nature. Once he has developed a character where these two poles are in harmony, he will be able to feel peaceful within himself. Then, based on this personal achievement, he can take the position of subject without transmitting anger and madness at the same time. With this maturity, he will not oppress those around him, but instead guide them to find ways to make harmony with each other. In this sense, if today friction passes within and between many human beings, it is because we choose to follow the program that promotes only one pole. As a consequence, our character is either subjective or objective and we cannot move between both positions according to our situation.

It seems quite obvious that in order to create a painting a painter has to use different colors and distinguish one paint stroke from another if he wants his work of art be considered beautiful. Nevertheless, in respect to our behavior we accept to 'paint' with only one pole and to disregard all other poles, which is like valuing only one color and creating a painting with just the color blue or the color red. Often, our thoughts are either in the category of all 'blue' or in the category of all 'red'. As time passes we create a character that stands for 'blue' all the time, or vice versa, just for 'red' all the time, or any other 'color' we identify ourselves with.

Nevertheless a person of only one 'color' is not recognized as being beautiful, and due to having developed only one part, he has great difficulty to transform his character, if he wishes to do so. When we observe ourselves, it seems that this tendency of valuing only one side is not just skin deep, but comes from deep within ourselves.

As we know, if within a family the parents always take a subjective role toward their child, this child is forced to continuously take an objective role. If he does not maintain that role, he will fight with his parents. On the other hand, if the parents tend to take an objective position towards everything and are always soft with their child, that child will develop a strong subjective nature and will not have difficulty to be very demanding to his parents.

Based on this reality we can say we are truly 'printed' with a program that contains a destructive purpose, which permits us to take only one side. Consequently we become part of either the submissive group or of the oppressive group and we develop our characters accordingly.

Finding our Original Purpose

But regardless of what history has shown to us and what positions we have been obliged to take, we need to remind ourselves that we have an original purpose, even though it might have been damaged. The main function of our original purpose is to value the duality between the subjective and the objective poles, allowing us to create life and beauty. Let's observe the duality between the Earth and the Sun. This miraculous duality allows some people to see a sunset while people in another part of the planet are seeing a sunrise! As we become a witness to this cosmic movement that permits life to exist, we come to comprehend the design of our own purpose. Like the program of the universe that guides this majestic planet Earth and all other planets, our original purpose is also guiding us to move in harmonious duality with everything that is around us. Therefore, if humans do not wish to reprogram their beings according to this cosmic design, they will always behave centering on one pole, which is like being only the nighttime or only the daytime. In other words, they will always mainfest either a subjective type of character or an objective type of character.

If we wish to see a different type of character developing within ourselves, a character that can alternate between the positions of subject and object, we need to first learn to see duality within everything we perceive. As we begin to recognize this duality, we 'print' something different inside our minds, which in time will influence the core of our being. To make an analogy, if we observe a tree, we will realize that the tree consists of a trunk, branches and leaves, and that these aspects display different colors of brown and green. And if we observe the duality among these different parts and their attributes, we might come to discover that we can know whether the tree is approaching its time of awakening, its time of full foliage, or its time of preparation for the winter.

As we know, for someone to speak a new language, he has to learn that language first. Regardless this is not easy, as he continues to practice, the day will come when he will be able to communicate his ideas through that language. Learning to see duality is just like learning another language. To acquire this 'language', just like with any other language, we have to practice it over and over; in this case, practice to see duality in all the different aspects of our life, like for example, when we take a walk in the park and look at a tree or a flower or any other aspect of the creation. By training our mind to see duality everywhere, we will see ourselves wanting to become creators of duality as well.

Today we spend so much time learning the individual names of different parts of the physical universe, their composition, properties, and so forth. Unfortunately we usually do not learn to see the duality between or within those different components. Until we can do that, we will not be able to fully understand the purpose of their existence, individually as well as collectively. It is like knowing there is a Sun, there is an Earth, there is a day and there is a night, but until we see the duality between all these aspects, we cannot perceive their purpose and connection, or find their ultimate value. In this sense, if we re-educate ourselves to see subjective as well as the objective poles and realize that they have equal importance for sustaining life, we will reconfigure the 'program' inside our minds and thereby begin to understand the purpose of our physical lives.

As well, by perceiving the world through the point of view that everything functions and is maintained based on the duality between different poles in the position of subject and the position of object, we will realize that the One who is the Origin of everything must also have this concept within Him/Herself. This is the reason this Origin was destined to create so much beauty in the many things we see around us. All of them contain this blueprint of duality within themselves, from the large scale, like all the planets that are rotating around the sun, to the small scale, like all the electrons that are turning around a nucleus. As we begin to perceive all these dualities existing around us, we can begin to comprehend that we, too, were created based on this blueprint and therefore we were meant to be in relationship with everything.

But due to another destructive program within ourselves, we are prevented from recognizing duality and obliged to choose just one pole from among all poles. Consequently we always feel we need to defend ourselves against other poles or attack them as if they were our enemies. For this reason, when someone tells us something that represents the view of another pole, we tend to reject whatever that person says. But when he tells us something that is similar to the pole that we have developed, we tend to accept whatever he says and agree with him, since it gives value to our pole. For example, if we have developed a subjective character and someone proposes that we join a strike so that some change can take place, we will consider this to be a good idea. We will easily agree with him because his plan is in accord with our character of aggression, of being in control, and so on. One the other hand, if we have developed an objective character and someone asks us to take a stand against something, we will have a difficult time to agree with that idea. It is not because there might be something wrong with this suggestion, but because we value passivity. Due the pole we have developed, we tend to not value this idea and eventually reject it, since it demands from us to take more initiative.

This might be a simple event, and yet this reality exists everywhere around us. Actually, we often perceive the pole someone represents before we even talk to that person. We naturally tend to choose a friend who has a more objective character when we want someone to not fight with us but to agree with us. In another case, as many of us might have experienced when going to some store, we might be reluctant to ask the attendant for something because we perceive that he or she has quite a subjective character and therefore will not easily accept to help us or might even reject us. According to our perception, we would prefer to go to someone who looks more accommodating.

Ideally, we would like to find an attendant who has both characteristics, objective and subjective, in balance within himself. The reason is, we hope this person will be able to switch his position according to what position we are taking in front of him. When we present our question, we hope he will take an objective position, and when we expect an answer, we hope he will take a subjective position. Yet we might experience that after listening to our question, the attendant takes an even more extreme position of the same pole. In other words, he is objective and listens to us, but in the process he becomes more and more objective, to the point that he says he does not know before we even finish asking our question. So, regardless we perceive that he did not show any aggression and therefore was a good person to approach, we surely did not expect him to take an even more objective position when we anticipated some direction from him.

Becoming Beautiful 'Fruit'

In general we can say, in order to create beauty, no matter if a person approaches someone else or if this person is approached by someone, we have to always maintain the concept of duality within our minds. In this sense, when someone speaks to us, we need to accept to listen to that person without believing because we listen we are oppressed. And when it is our turn to speak, we need to do so without wanting to dominate the other person. As explained, the way to create beauty is to learn to switch our position according to the demand of the situation. If we keep choosing one pole and denying the other pole, we cannot create beauty nor feel we ourselves are beautiful. Only by making effort every day to perceive and create duality in every circumstance, we can begin to print a new program in ourselves and start to fulfill the purpose we were created with, which is to become beautiful for others.

As well, when we begin to experience seeing two poles instead of one, we will also begin to perceive the Creator of everything and His/Her nature. We will realize that this Creator must have similar characteristics to what is existing around us. For example, like a flower, He/She must have a mind that is just as delicate as a petal or as pure and brilliant as a drop of water on this flower. As we begin to recognize our Creator, we will increase the awareness of our own selves as being part of His/Her creation. We will begin to perceive the dualities within our own being and we will realize we are meant to maintain countless dualities in order to fulfill our purpose of goodness, or become 'fruits' of goodness.

Even if we realize we were designed to become 'fruits' of goodness, this belief does not guarantee that our minds will operate according to that design. Surely, God intended human beings to have minds that would look for duality, as does the rest of the creation. But since we have lost the program that teaches that joy can only come to exist when we are in harmony with everything around us, we are unable to follow a way of life that would allow us to exist in continuous joy and peace. Based on this reality, we surely need to review our philosophy, if we wish to be part of the universal beauty. Maybe we believe we are all meant to live together in harmony, but at the same time we need to be aware that our minds are filled with many destructive thoughts that prevent us from making duality with what comes into our lives and thus prevents us from creating peace. The reality is that we have developed our characters based on a single or an egocentric pole. For this reason we have immense difficulties to see and to create beauty and we have established a world based on self-survival, self-defense and self-interest instead.

Our hope today is that we can recreate minds that are divine, which means minds that represent God's Mind, in order to fulfill the purpose that God intended for us. Surely if God could see us becoming persons that are in harmony within ourselves and with others, He/She could recognize us as part of the creation and at the same time we could be part of God. How can we become these kinds of persons? As we have mentioned previously, in order to install new programs inside our 'microchips', we need to focus on seeing duality in everything existing around us. When looking at something we should ask ourselves, "What is the subjective or objective part of what I see?" These attributes could include the colors, the shapes or the sounds of the object. After finding one pole, we can begin to look for the opposite pole. As we practice doing this we will be able to re-print the original program inside our beings and remove whatever is not following this original program.

In this sense, if we tend to look only for the subjective aspect of what we see, it means we need to make effort to look at the objective aspect as well and learn to value this pole as much as we value the subject pole. Likewise, if we are persons who usually value the objective aspect, we have to learn to also value the subjective aspect, if we want to create a new mechanism in ourselves. Otherwise, due to the program that is already installed in us, we will always have a tendency to reject what is around us and friction will be inevitable.

We need to learn to switch our positions according to what we perceive is happening around us. If someone speaks to us we need to take the object position of listening to that person. If we cannot do that and we want to speak at the same time as the other person is speaking, this desire will provoke conflict in us and with others.

In the process of learning to develop the dual characteristics of subject and object within ourselves, it will become more and more easy for us to make harmonious relationships with others. We will be able to change more easily from the subject position to the object position and vice versa, and in the process harmony and beauty will begin to exist within and around us.

The law of duality applies to groups as well as to individual persons. If a group of people with passive characters meets another group with the same characteristics, they will not be able to communicate with each other because no one will initiate anything. These two objective groups cannot progress in their relationships, since both groups did not develop the subjective sides of their characters that would permit them to build ideas or perform actions, instead of retreating within themselves, saying, "I do not know what to say" or "I do not know what to do." Interestingly, objective people look calmer than those who have subjective characters, nevertheless due to their inability to come out of themselves they often carry deep frustration and have low self-esteem, which makes them feel depressed to a higher degree than the subjective group.

The bottom line is, no matter which pole we develop, the subjective or the objective part within our characters, one thing is for sure: we will not find happiness, or if we do experience happiness, it will not last for long. If human beings cannot follow the path of achieving harmony between their objective and subjective characteristics, their only common point will be the struggle and frustration that they all recognize in and between each other.

Although this point of view might not look scientific because it deals with the world of emotion, which cannot easily be measured, it actually is scientific. According to science, energy is created based on two poles relating in harmony with each other. As well, based on their harmonious relationship development begins, which helps to maintain matter and, above all, create energy. If this principle of harmony is applied in the lives of human beings, we can observe the more we follow this law the more we are able to maintain the integrity of our characters, create the energy of love and mature ourselves.

Yet many times human beings do not behave according to the laws of physics. They are not always seeking to relate with other poles in the same way as their physical bodies maintain their existences based on the laws of duality. Ultimately, human beings are following a philosophy of trying to not surrender to other poles and trying to be independent from other poles. Regardless that the viewpoint of being independent seems to be something positive, we also know, if protons wanted to be independent from electrons, we surely would not have the same creation as we can observe today. Instead we would see everything turning to dust or nothing being created in the first place. In human beings as well, following the philosophy of trying to be independent from each other promotes emptiness and destruction.

Scientists know that everything concerning the mechanisms of matter, from the smallest to the largest scale, functions based on the duality between different poles. Therefore, when these scholars observe human beings who are not living according to the principles of science and demonstrating so much aggression, they might quickly understand why people carry so much sickness and depression.

From all this we can conclude, regardless of what pole we choose to promote, if we stand only for the subjective pole, we will end up fighting with others and making our own hearts miserable, and if we uphold the objective pole, we will find ourselves becoming bored and many other feelings connected to that. To use an analogy, are we interested in creating a garden where only a few plants can survive or do we prefer to create a garden that is filled up with many blooming plants? Surely, if we want to have a beautiful garden, the first thing we have to agree on is that we need many different kinds of flowers. And then we will have to think about how we are going to display each color with other colors. Based on this consideration and study, we can create a garden that is so beautiful that it will attract everyone who is in town to visit. Based on the blueprint of duality needed to make a lovely garden, by making duality with many poles we will be able to elevate ourselves and become persons who are so beautiful that many people will be attracted to us and will try to find ways to come close to us.

The Problem of Good and Evil

The point of duality is not to evalutate whether the characteristic of subject or the characteristic of object is better, but to find how these two characteristics can relate in harmony with each other. Today, even though human beings wish to live in harmony, based on their minds that are programmed with a destructive purpose, they keep looking for the good and the bad in everything they see and do. Whatever they choose to value they will consider as good, and whatever they reject they will consider as bad. For example, someone with a subjective character who finds himself having to listen to someone will not think this is something that is good for him. He considers the quality of listening as an undesirable trait, to the point that he judges the person who asks him to listen. Due to this perception, a small incident can turn into a huge fight. Vice versa, if someone who has an objective character is asked to say something, that person will reject that demand and eventually reject the one who wanted him to speak as not understanding or respecting him, to the point of also judging him. To eliminate this concept of good or bad and the preference of one pole over others, it would be wise for human beings to begin to choose the philosophy of valuing the necessity of two poles. Only by maintaining this thought will they be guaranteed to be perceived as lovely persons all the time.

If for example we consider the color black as bad, no one will choose the color black, because no one wants to be identified as a bad person. And if tomorrow we choose the color white as bad, no one will choose the color white, because everyone will be afraid of being accused to like white. For this reason, in order to create peace as well as beauty, we need to learn to accept and combine many different colors in our lives. Otherwise, similar to choosing one color as good and others as bad, if we only value the qualities of initiating and making decisions, everybody will want to become a subjective type of person. But this means that everyone will want to talk and initiate ideas and no one will want to listen, fearing to be judged as bad.

In any case, if we value only one pole or consider only one pole as a reference of what is good, this will involve us in many conflicts. Let us imagine there would be only one pole, like the North Pole, then what would happen to this planet Earth? One scenario would be that all the magnetic energy of the planet would go to that one pole, which would play havoc with our climate. If there were conflict between the North Pole and the South Pole, one phenomenon we might perceive is the ocean changing its level or transforming its currents. Surely if this happened, it would affect many other things, for example, it would confuse the fish that are living in the ocean, causing them to no longer know what direction they should go. To readjust themselves to their changing environment and to be able to survive, they would have to reprogram all their inner codes, if they have an option to do so.

If we envision our planet looking like this, then we are surely glad these possibilities did not become realities. We have to truly acknowledge that because our planet has two major poles existing in harmony, it is an extremely pleasant place to live.

But because the destructive program inside human beings makes us blind to others, when we come together it impossible for us to know what roles we should play. This is the reason that the most difficult thing on this Earth seems to be to communicate with each other, even just to exchange simple ideas. Because our destructive program values only one pole instead of two poles, we are always busy trying to figure out which pole is good and which pole is bad, according to our own self-interest, instead of trying to create harmonious relationships with other poles. And once we have identified which pole is good, we feel we have to defend ourselves against the influence of any other pole. Due to this egocentric point of view, we believe we should not make any relationship with whatever we consider to be a bad pole, to make sure we do not get 'contaminated'.

In fact, this tendency of overvaluing ourselves and being in fear of every other pole is what we have seen taking place all throughout history. One group of people has always identified itself as good and considered the other group, which includes everyone else, as bad. The ones who are considered to be bad do the same by declaring themselves as good and identifying everyone else as bad.

Based on this view we can easily understand how groups who each represent different poles or ideas perpetually come to look at each other as enemies. If someone within one group has a specific idea and expresses it to his own group, they will always view his idea as good. However, if this same person goes to the other group with his idea, surely it will not be easy for his idea to be welcomed, because any idea that the other pole initiates is automatically considered to be bad. From this we can realize a new idea is often rejected because any group or individual, no matter who they are, does not value surrendering to another group or individual. The only way they can agree with one another is by one side taking an objective position, which of course is usually unacceptable to either side. Since each human being wants to maintain his superiority, it is understandable why each instinctually does not welcome any proposal from another pole, regardless it might be something good for everyone.

Evolution Through Harmony

What if all electrons considered only themselves as good and based on this static viewpoint judged all the protons as representatives of what is bad, and vice versa? Then instead of turning around each other in order to create atoms, both sides would begin to attack each other until one side was exhausted. If there were this constant harassment between particles, would we consider that the God who made the creation is a God who has a character of goodness? In order to have friction and opposition instead of harmony in His creation, God would have needed to create one pole as good and the other as evil so that they would repel each other. And He would have been aware that sooner or later the Earth would stop to exist or never exist in the first place, since based on such a theory everything disintegrates. Regardless we might want to believe that the God who created this Earth and who influences human beings is the kind of God who initiated the idea that progress comes through revolution, we cannot uphold this concept, because the world would have destroyed itself even before we as human beings had a chance to 'arrive' on it. Therefore we can only conclude, if God is good, which we can perceive through the laws of harmony that exist within the creation, then someone else besides God must have printed a program in human beings that encourages selectiveness and destruction. Consequently human beings are fulfilling this other purpose, which makes them continuously fight, frequently under the paradoxical belief of bringing about evolution.

In order to change our destructive program, which eventually makes us reject even our own selves, we have to study and acknowledge the laws of physics, chemistry and biology that allow the flowers to become beautiful. When we observe them and all other living things, we will realize their virtue is to accept every pole around them. To achieve this will take some effort from our part, if we want to become beautiful like other living things. Because we are so focused on choosing what is good and what is bad and make this our priority, we do not perceive the way to become beautiful and mature and instead we keep searching fruitlessly for how to be beautiful or peaceful.

Usually we start looking for beauty in our bodies or our skin. And if we succeed in making our bodies or our skin beautiful, we still feel this is not it. Subsequently, we will try to find beauty within our minds through education. And when we find some kind of beauty within our minds based on choosing a certain philosophy, we again do not feel satisfied. Then we will look for beauty within our hearts, hoping this will allow us to truly feel we are beautiful. So indeed, to make ourselves beautiful is a gigantic task for us human beings, because we are made with many dimensions. Therefore, we have to achieve several levels of beauty before we can be viewed as truly beautiful by others and ourselves.

If we study our thinking, we will discover the root of all the thoughts that bring about conflicts within and subsequently between human beings, ultimately comes from valuing ourselves, the 'I', as the only legitimate pole. Understandably, whatever idea follows based on the viewpoint of this 'I' is considered to be 'right' while everything else is considered to be 'wrong'. Accordingly, when another pole initiates a thought, since this thought is not just a neutral idea but also introduces the possibility that there is another 'I' besides us, it automatically creates a reaction within our

'I' and therefore that person's view will be considered to be 'wrong'.

Human beings seem to be so imprinted with the philosophy of the 'I' that it seems there is no way to ever welcome another pole. It looks like we are destined to glorify ourselves and curse others. In order for a person who has been carrying the program of the 'I' to be able to relate harmoniously with another person, this person must go through some metamorphosis that permits him to become a 'dualistic person', or we can also say, a person of the number two instead of a person of the number one. Two of such people together can no longer be referred to as single persons, instead they need to be recognized as plural or as 'we'.

We need to be aware that as long as the root of the 'I' is imprinted inside our 'microchip', we are forced to dwell upon that 'I' all throughout our lives. If we ask that 'I', "How big are you? How many megabytes do you occupy? How much is the purpose of my life to fulfill your wish? Will I be beautiful just by being loyal to you, the 'I'?", the 'I' will answer, "You have to understand that your existence is based on the original 'I'. The way to know who you are is to fulfill the desires of the 'I'."

But can an electron fulfill the purpose of its life alone or is it because it has a relationship with a proton that it can sustain its own existence and at the same time create something bigger? Can an electron say that it is beautiful when it is alone? Or is it when it makes a relationship with a proton that it can be considered to be beautiful?

How about us? What is our original divine purpose? Surely it cannot be what we have just described, always emphasizing only one pole, which essentially means continuously promoting the 'I'. Instead of fulfilling the wish of the 'I' as our primary goal, human beings must have a purpose similar to the atomic world that the scientists teach us about, which consists of one particle being in relationship with another particle. This means, if we want to create life and beauty, each individual human being has to find another human being. It is like when we see a blossom, we tend to look for the leaves or branches or something else around this blossom as well, and as we perceive the duality between the blossom, its leaves and its branches, we consider this to be a flower in its complete beauty.

In this sense, we perceive beauty when we find another pole besides the one we see first. For example, there is the sun that brings the light of the day after the darkness, and there is the moon that brings light in the middle of the darkness, and both are valuable. As we learn to perceive duality everywhere, we become beautiful mentally, which allows us to receive energy. Once we achieve this dimension of beauty, then we can look for a higher dimension, which is the dimension of emotion. This means, after human beings can create mental serenity within themselves, they are ready to go to the level of emotion, which, simply said, is the level of love. And if love can become part of us, we surely won't have difficulty to recognize this dimension existing all around us. In this sense, as we develop all these dimensions of beauty within ourselves, which are the body, the mind and the heart, we can be considered to be human beings who can live three-dimensional lives, not flat lives.

Then if we meet someone who also has developed the dimensions of the body, the mind, and the heart, our relationship of giving and receiving will allow both of us to receive life to the fullest degree, and at that time we can truly say that we are happy. As well, the people who are around us will perceive absolute beauty when they look at us, and by relating with us they will receive nourishment. If we again compare this with the atomic world of protons and electrons or of positive and negative ions, we can also see they not only maintain themselves but they create life or energy on a bigger scale as well. As we witness this extremely majestic phenomenon, we can surely understand, if human beings want to rediscover and fulfill their original purpose, which is to create life on all different levels, they have to reconsider what they value as good and evil. If they label one pole as good and another pole as evil, they isolate themselves from each other and create conflict, which destroys the energy that was meant to exist between them. As a result they block life for themselves as well as for those who are next to them. The moment we start to analyze the effect of dividing everything between good and bad, we will realize this perception ultimately makes us advocate only ourselves, to the point of destroying everyone else while at the same time preventing our own development.

The One Who Recognized Every Pole

We might ask if throughout the long course of human history someone ever existed who, instead of promoting only his own pole, was promoting life and therefore carrying life within his own self? We can know that there must have been someone like this, because if not, no one would choose to refer to another human being as their Shepherd, their Master or their Lord, to the point of being willing to follow this person.

If we look at this personage who was considered to have life, we will realize that inside the 'microchip' of his mind he must no longer have had the program that promotes only valuing one pole and always rejecting the other pole. This individual must have found a new theory, different from the theories so often practiced on this Earth that say in order to survive one pole has to attack another pole. When we observe this person's life, we can see he always promoted the view of valuing others as much as himself, and that he worked hard to maintain his theory of harmony between poles. If he had not chosen to promote a different theory than the one that is prevalent in this world, he could not have had life and would not have been confident to say he would go to a place where life was eternal, but instead he would have said that the world was a place of eternal emptiness.

Therefore this person must have had the correct thinking in order to be able to fulfill his original divine purpose and to have eternal life. He must have discovered that making duality with others, which we usually refer to as 'loving others', is crucial in order to have life, and that rejecting others condemns us to no longer have life, or we can also say, to live in a place where there is only a desert. Surely, I will say that this person whom many call their Lord must have been a philosopher of divinity, who not only thought well but also tried to achieve what he believed in. And based on his constructive thought he could develop the third dimension within himself, which we consider to be the heart. We can assume in order to create a heart that resembled what the God in Heaven wished to see in humans, this person must have practiced the theory of respecting every pole, no matter if it came from the North, the South, the East or the West. In doing so he could reach a point where he could no longer see evil in this world but only see the potential goodness in everything.

As I introduce this Lord, whom we call Jesus, I want to also state that in his lifetime the theory of accepting every pole was not so popular, especially by the ones who considered that the absolute right thing to do on this Earth was to imprison, enslave, or stone the ones whom they did not like. Regardless of these circumstances, this Lord was not tempted to act upon these concepts. And when the people educated by the theory of valuing only one pole and removing every other pole came to him asking what they should do when someone sinned, saying, "Teacher, this woman was caught in the act of adultery. In the Law Moses commanded us to stone such women. Now what do you say?" (John 8:4-6), he would not agree with their concept. He knew if the North Pole rejects the South Pole, the North Pole alone cannot survive regardless the South Pole might look like the living devil.

Surely we can see that this Lord, who is also called the Shepherd, was a new human being who carried the program of God within himself. He was aware that two poles coming together in perfect harmony could make us perceive beauty and at the same time create ourselves as beautiful beings. For this reason he drove himself every day of his life to fulfill his original divine purpose, practicing to recognize everyone and everything as being important and necessary in order to create life, regardless he knew the people around him did not perceive their surroundings in the same way as he did. They did not value the same theory as he did, which is expressed in the verse, "So in everything, do to others what you would have them do to you, for this sums up the Law and the Prophets" (Matt. 7:12). Eventually he was attacked by them, yet he did not fight back as they might have expected. He knew that those who made divisions between good and evil had no life. This is the reason he said to his Father in heaven, "Father, forgive them, for they do not know what they are doing" (Luke 23:34).

As we continue to look at this Lord called Jesus, we can only be amazed by him. He never acted upon the concept of 'righteousness', which many times forces us to promote only one pole, but he only acted upon the concept that everyone has to live, no matter who they are. He was persistent in welcoming everyone. He knew that any person who did not create life within his flesh and soul could not live where God dwelled, but instead he would carry remorse for eternity, until he could find a way to regain life.

Jesus' Loyalty to the Law of Life

So regardless there were those around him who were always tempting him to make choices between right and wrong, he did not give in to them. He knew that when we choose one category of thought as being right and another as being wrong, this only provokes hostility. In this case, instead of creating the positive energy necessary to have life, we build negative energy, which leads to emptiness. He was also aware if he chose to support one pole, people would consider him to be a revolutionary and use his example for the purpose of making conflict. Contrary to their wishes, he promoted the theory of giving to every side what belonged to them: "Give to Caesar what is Caesar's, and to God what is God's" (Matt. 22:21). And instead of attacking the ones who were considered not good or removing someone from the planet Earth because this person appeared sinful in the eyes of the people, he promoted forgiveness, hoping that the one who was forgiven would choose a new pattern of life. Through this way of teaching we truly can see the Lord Jesus acknowledged every person around him, even though he did not agree with the theory they carried because he knew their theory did not create the energy of life that was necessary to create beauty and divinity every day.

If the Shepherd or Lord had given into the temptation of choosing according to the traditional right and wrong, and condemning everyone who did not agree with the pole he supported, he would not have been able to give hope to anyone. If he had judged any other pole, believing that he was doing the right thing, he would have demonstrated that he was incapable of loving every human being. Worst of all, by doing so he would have condemned himself at the same time, because he would have been unable to receive the love from God that made him divine.

Through the way of life of the one we call the Shepherd or the Lord, we can realize he was extremely ingenious in understanding his purpose and he was extremely wise in maintaining his integrity, never wavering from the path of striving to fulfill his purpose. Many times he repeated his message, "Do not judge, or you too will be judged. For in the same way you judge others, you will be judged, and with the measure you use, it will be measured to you" (Matt. 7:1-2). With these words he demonstrated that he knew when we judge someone, we are expelling the pole that is necessary for us to create the relationship that will sustain life within and between us.

Surely, this Lord understood the process of life very well, regardless that science was not as much developed in his time as it is today. He had a chance to observe how the lizard was sleeping when it was alone and, when there were many lizards, how they ran together and created energy. Based on all the knowledge he had gained through his environment, the Lord taught through parables that by accepting other poles, human beings are actually loving themselves as well, because through this they are able to receive the elements of life that ultimately permit them to create the Kingdom of Heaven on this Earth. This is the reason he said, "The Kingdom of God does not come with your careful observation, nor will people say, 'Here it is,' or 'There it is,' because the Kingdom of God is within you" (Luke 17:20-21). We can also say that this Lord was trying to prevent human beings from becoming thirsty and starving in the dimension of their souls. He knew if our souls were starving in this life, we would continue to be hungry in our eternal lives until we had learned to follow the principles of life. If the people around him had followed what he taught and recognized him as their pole, they could have understood and thus followed the concept of duality, which would have allowed them to gain life. They could have matured themselves and become the first citizens of the Kingdom of Heaven, in the lifetime of this Lord.

Yet instead, the people around him chose to follow the program that they had inherited from history, which was to value only themselves and to reject everyone else. They did not want to listen to the message the Lord brought to them and chose to argue with him in order to keep their 'I' as the only pole. They refused to honor him as their rabbi, and even less, to recognize him as the most important person of their time. And as they maintained the root of the 'I' in his presence, they attempted to dismiss what he taught and eventually to dismiss even him. This is the reason that it became so difficult for following generations to know who he really was.

Nevertheless, as we know now, if one atom rejects another one, energy and life cannot be sustained or created and therefore we will have difficulty to recognize this event as something great. In the same manner, if a group of individuals chooses to remove another individual, regardless they believe they are right in what they are doing, it will also be difficult to recognize their action as a good thing, since it destroys life. In this sense, regardless of what blessing people wish to receive, they will be blessed based on the theory they follow and thus they will reap sweetness or regret and sorrow.

Based on what we know about the Lord Jesus from the Scriptures or historical records, we can say he was a person who embodied this principle of life. Regardless people invited him to be their friend and to adopt their theories, he was loyal to fulfilling the purpose of his divine mind in accordance with the laws by which God created this world. Based on this difference between him and the people around him, as illustrated when he said, "You are from below; I am from above. You are of this world; I am not of this world" (John 8:23), we can imagine he must have had great difficulties to have any friends at all, especially when these 'friends' asked him to take their views of separating from other poles. While others were asking him to reject someone else in order to elevate their own value, the Lord considered others as the base for making relationships in order to create life. For him the thought of removing another pole was the same as rejecting the Creator of the flower and just seeing the flower by itself.

Through these great differences on the level of mind and heart, surely the Lord must have felt deeply that he was not understood by the people around him and he must have realized that living on this Earth surely did not resemble living in the Kingdom of Heaven. And at a crucial moment in his life he said, "My kingdom is not of this world. If it were, my servants would fight to prevent my arrest by the Jews. But now my kingdom is from another place" (John 18:36). After searching in vain to find a friend who could understand him, we can imagine that he must have questioned what purpose the people of his day were pursuing in their lives, since whatever they were thinking was always connected to removing someone or something. And as they kept thinking about getting rid of someone, surely the actual deed was not too far away.

The Shepherd and Lord many times must have been shocked and perplexed about the people around him, especially when they became violent, and paradoxically, at the same time they would be afraid of what would happen to them after their physical lives. Regardless of how violent they had become, he would also see them trying to find some remedy for the atrocities they committed by going to the temple. They performed specific ceremonies in order to remove their sin, which they must have blamed as the cause for their violence.

Different from them, the Shepherd and Lord did not advocate the necessity of performing all the ceremonies that the Jewish and Roman people had initiated. This means he must have had some other cure to remove the origin of our violence, some other way that could help us to change the program inside ourselves which caused us to perform actions of destruction. And indeed, his approach, perceivable through what he taught his followers, was to consider everything that was living around him to be important. By following this way, we would be able to reprogram ourselves and thus destroy whatever triggered us to become so violent.

A Sheep Among Wolves

This Lord was convinced that by making duality with everything, he could create divine life, for himself as well as for the people who were willing to relate with him. He knew if we could not follow his principle of peace, another law would be installed, one where human beings acted like wolves that approached sheep, not to create the energy of life, but to devour them for their own satisfaction. This is what he meant when he said to some of his followers, "I am sending you out like sheep among wolves. Therefore be as shrewd as snakes and as innocent as doves" (Matt. 10:16). He gave this advice in order to help his disciples to keep their innocence, in other words, to stay loyal to the principle of duality which he was so loyal to.

Jesus knew that those portrayed as wolves were also in jeopardy, because the more they acted against the theory of harmony, the more they would become involved with the principle of destruction and thus the farther away from the possibility of being redeemed from their madness and violence, even in small matters. Being blinded by their madness they could not perceive what God wanted to give to them, in other words, they would not be able to recognize the One who came as their Shepherd and consequently would truly turn into 'wolves'. They would attack those who were with the Shepherd, believing that he was wrong and he did not come to bring peace, but to provoke war. More than that, they would even try to remove him. And in the end they would be alone again, only with their angry selves.

This ultimate tragedy eventually took place because of people who had chosen themselves as the central and the only poles that had the right to exist, which amplified the negativity that was already printed inside the programs of their minds. This thought that they were the only ones who were right became so dominant that it took over every one of their cells and turned them violent. If, instead of following the commands of the destructive program inside them, they had humbled themselves before the Shepherd and listened to him, they would have been able to be engrafted with a new program and thus receive new guidance, which in time would have allowed them to resemble Jesus.

For this reason today, after two millennia, at a time when we still recognize Jesus as our Shepherd and our Lord, we should not just glorify him as the one who has life and as the one who has the right to go to a place where life is eternal, but we should also learn to print his thought inside our minds in order to change the program that demands us to follow our egocentric desires. As well, if human beings do not consider it necessary to follow the actual path that the Lord Jesus has taken and if they are only content to praise him for what he has achieved, I do not think they will have as much redemption or salvation as they are promised. It is not by applauding our Lord to be the winner but by taking the same road as he and by building ourselves with divine minds and bodies that we can develop life, to the point we can be recognized by him as his friends. This is the reason we need to follow him instead of just always wanting to be forgiven by him. Furthermore, if each one of us can become a person of life, then I think the Lord will surely be happy to share his heart with us. Nevertheless, in order for that to happen, human beings have to truly educate their minds based on the original root of divine thought, which is that everything that has life has the principle of duality as its foundation.

Therefore as explained, in order to abandon the monopoly of the 'I' that presents itself as the only one who is right, which of course makes every one else wrong, we have to learn to recognize other poles as being as important as our own pole. Nevertheless, if we only make that transformation intellectually, our relationships with others will not be automatically transformed, because a relationship entails a specific thought as well as a specific action. In this sense, if we are just content to educate our minds, this effort alone will not make us qualified to receive the same blessing of divinity as our Shepherd and Lord acquired. In order to receive the blessing to create life for ourselves and to eventually to give life to others, we have to practice this view of duality on a daily basis, which will allow us to transform what is dark in us into light. In the process our relationships will become harmonious and we will begin to perceive a sweetness within our characters. Most of all, the more we venture along this path, the more we will discover the true nature of the Shepherd, our Lord, which at the same time will permit us to become aware of the depth of his heart.

Even if the person who is next to you does not choose the theory of valuing both poles, he still might enjoy being with someone who is making a lot of effort to create duality. But even though this person experiences some happiness because he is next to someone who practices the law of duality, at the end of his life this individual will find his destiny is not the same as the destiny of the one who tried throughout his life to create duality with everyone around him.

In this sense, when the Lord Jesus was with the people of his time, he did not tell them where they would be after their lives here on Earth, maybe because he did not want to scare them. He only told them that they would not be living with him in the Kingdom of Heaven: "Not everyone who says to me, 'Lord, Lord,' will enter the kingdom of heaven, but only he who does the will of my Father who is in heaven" (Matt. 7:21). Surely, Jesus made this statement because he knew human beings are not only elevated by believing in some ideal, however great it could be, but to truly be transformed and to become divine we need to follow an extraordinary road.

Daily Transformation with Jesus

If human beings want to follow the universal law, they need to understand that the path they have to take is different from just believing in a great ideal, regardless this also demands effort. Therefore, even though this Lord would have valued a person who had elevated his or her mind by choosing the Lord's thoughts, which brings change within one's mental dimension, the Lord also knew if people's ideals do not connect with what they do every day, they cannot purify the dimension of their flesh. Only by practicing their ideals, their bodies can become more and more obedient and transparent, to the point that their flesh is as pure as their minds. This is the reason this Lord said that we need to become like children. It is only then that we can experience complete harmony within ourselves, like he did.

Indeed, if we listen to our Shepherd, we can see he was not just content to make us believe in him. Instead he continuously encouraged people to follow the same road as he had followed in order to make sure that they would gain life as he had life. But it seems this desire was not so popular among the people who were with him. They were expecting miracles, which means they must have held a philosophy that did not demand any effort from their part. Even though the Lord Jesus did perform many miracles, at the same time he gave guidance on how to build divine identities and to not only believe in him. In fact, he walked with his friends through many situations in order to show them how to live their lives.

It might look complicated for human beings to embody the idea of valuing every pole for its potential role in making a relationship. This is the reason we might prefer to follow those who preach that only believing in an ideal of a great person is necessary in order to be redeemed. Regardless of what we consider to be our difficulty, until we focus on living according to what our Shepherd, our Lord, recognized as valuable, we cannot even begin to experience the relationship he had with his Father in Heaven. As well, unless we can find his heart, it will be difficult for us to present ourselves before him when we come to the end of our physical lives and begin our lives in the spiritual world.

When we observe a scientist, we can see that he researches all the microscopic and macroscopic worlds because he wants to know the secret of how everything functions. He does all this research not in order to be superior to everyone who does not have this knowledge but in order to remove humanity's ignorance, thereby reducing the external difficulties and sicknesses of human beings. Likewise, if human beings research the original purpose of their lives, not just because they are incapable of managing their lives but because they want to live to their fullest potential, this will permit them to discover the process by which they can build within themselves what their Shepherd had built within himself.

Then the question is, what road will we take? Will it be the road that the Shepherd and Lord Jesus Christ invited all of humankind to take so they would be able to have life as he had life? Or will it be the road that some other people promote, which is the road of rebelling against and rejecting other poles? Based on our choice of road, we will see different 'fruits' within ourselves at the end of our lives. If the fruit is good, we can assume the tree it came from must also be good and therefore the root of this tree must be good also. On the other hand, if the fruit is bitter or inedible, we need to accept the fact that the tree it came from did not receive the same nourishment as the tree that yielded delicious sweet fruits. What tree do we wish to be, a tree that is dead, a tree that can barely survive, or a tree that has life? We can assume the one who taught us to love others, eventually even our enemies – "But I tell you who hear me: Love your enemies, do good to those who hate you" (Luke 6:27) – must have understood how to become a tree of life. This is the reason he accepted everyone who was around him, regardless of his or her stature, background or reputation.

As we observe the way of life of our Shepherd and Lord we surely might want to 'wake up' and desire to live for others in order to be part of the realm where energy and life is created. In that dimension we will receive the life elements that will nourish our internal being and allow us to become mature so that one day we can be trees of life also. In this sense, regardless we might be alone in our wish of being a tree of life, we will become champions of duality. Contrary to that, if we wait for others to choose duality, we might be waiting and waiting, which means we will lose precious time here on Earth. Therefore, instead of waiting for someone to choose the same philosophy as we have, it is better for us to begin to take the road of our Shepherd and Lord right away.

And, if we dare to put our feet inside the footsteps of our Lord, we will realize he asks us to live with people who do not choose his philosophy. During his own life he intended to inspire those around him to use his philosophy and to follow his actions, but they did not. Regardless of this sad reality, he maintained the idea that life is created based on our relationships with others, not only between him and his Father but also between him and the people, and he never wavered from this principle.

Of course our Shepherd and Lord knew if people are constantly accusing and attacking what is around them, they are actually cursing and predestining themselves to be unable to receive the element of life, which is the fundamental nourishment for their souls to reach maturity. Since those around him refused to follow the law of love, he always found himself having to forgive them. He was patient with them because he knew that eventually they would suffer, be tired and unhappy, if not already here on this Earth then in their life afterwards. Realizing that he lived this way we can truly say, this Shepherd was a wise individual who understood that life and love were more important than differentiating between the people who were around him, whatever these persons did or did not do. He was aware that he had to create life at all costs in order for him to be victorious in the eyes of God.

Finding Jesus at the End of the Path

If this path he opened attracts us, we might have to honor what we have not honored so far. And if we decide to take this path, we might have to ask forgiveness from the one who came to give life, but who was rejected from the time he came to this Earth. After making this resolution and wanting to be graduated as true human beings, we will have to begin to respect other persons as we respect ourselves.

Our Lord wanted to make the people of his time discover the importance of their lives on Earth. This was because he knew the Earth was the only place where we could nourish ourselves to become citizens of a new 'land', also referred to as the Kingdom of Heaven, which we all somehow long for. He knew that this kingdom was actually based on purifying our flesh. In this sense, if people began to value the principle of relating with each other, they would cultivate this Kingdom where all citizens could breathe and be surrounded by life and love.

Maybe now is it understandable what Jesus meant when he said, "…the Son of Man did not come to be served, but to serve…" (Matt. 20:28). Surely the Shepherd, our Lord, did not consider that the Kingdom of Heaven was somewhere in an unapproachable place, but he knew that the Kingdom of Heaven was to be created deep within ourselves based on following the law of duality.

In the moment we begin to realize living for someone else is more enjoyable than living just for ourself, we will truly comprehend that the Kingdom our Lord described is very different from the world we are now living in. To establish this Kingdom we will surely need to accept to follow in his footsteps and, as we take this path, we will find him at the end of our road. Then we will not have to ask for forgiveness from him because we did not understand him, but we will meet him with a heart of joy because we became like him.

We can classify this belief as the true religion because it will lead us to fulfill our most divine purpose. As we follow this religion which teaches us to choose to value each pole, we will be able to re-program ourselves with the program that God has intended for us but we have somehow lost ever since the beginning of humanity. Indeed, if we choose this belief, we will realize by taking the road of giving everything to those who do not have, in return we are gaining the blessing of life.

As we know there are many different religions. Most of them glorify their own groups as special, in hope of attracting many people to their poles. However, in the process of overvaluing their own religion, which of course implies devaluing other religions to the point of advocating they should be removed, they separate. And as we now know, this egocentric view eventually diminishes life within those groups, since they punish themselves by not being part of the cosmic energy.

Indeed, we can say the simple theory of the North and South Poles truly shows us the secret to life. Millions of situations show us that in order for something to exist, there needs to be one pole in the subject position and another pole in the object position. Through this discovery we will also come to admire the One who organized this process and recognize how much He must have loved to see life. Indeed, the One who printed this law of duality in all the living things of creation, surely is a very special Creator.

Becoming Peacemakers

Accordingly, if within a family every individual is aware that each member represents one pole and he respects every other pole as he respects himself, then life energy will be perceivable within this family and we will consider this family to be beautiful. Likewise, if all human beings of this world are interested in creating a planet where everyone can receive life, then the multitude of groups that are separated from each other will have to re-evaluate what they stand for and what others represent for them. If every religious group could value and respect all other religious groups, the life elements of the universal God could truly begin to come to this planet. If they indeed all tried to create harmony with each other, this world would truly become a place where nobody lives in fear any more, but where instead everyone would live with peace in their hearts. Subsequently, as we all become responsible to live according to the law of duality, the energy of Heaven can come to each human being, no matter which group they belong to, and they all will begin to feel the love of Heaven for each other.

Nevertheless, when the Shepherd, our Lord, came to this Earth and he began to approach the religious people in positions of power, instead of welcoming him as a peacemaker, they viewed him as a war maker. Through this experience he realized the religious leaders were not in accord with the principle of God, which advocates looking for ways to harmonize with every situation in order to create life. Contrary to that, these leaders were quick to oppose him and his followers, as when they accused him, "He is possessed by Beelzebub! By the prince of demons he is driving out demons" (Mark 3:22).

If instead the religious groups could accept every other pole as having the same value as they themselves, especially since they are the ones who claim to believe that we need to love others, they surely would be able to receive what they all dream about, which is the love of God. Therefore, if this planet does not yet have life, it is because all the theologians and philosophers did not yet choose to carry the program that directs them to fulfill their original divine purpose, but instead they continue to follow the program that ask them to reject life.

Once human beings start to become tired of 'living' without life or become tired of just dreaming about receiving love, then I think they might begin to look for the way of life that will permit them to have the elements so vital for them, regardless these elements seem invisible to them. If human beings come to the conclusion that even though they have life physically, they still need to find the way to receive the energy of life in order for their souls to mature, they might accept to train themselves to live according to the law of the atoms, which demands an existence for a greater purpose than oneself. If we can do that with all of our awareness, knowledge and wisdom, then, like the Shepherd, our Lord, we, too, will able to say one day, "I am the way and the truth and the life" (John 14:6) and "Anyone who has seen me has seen the Father…" (John 14:9).

The Path of Life

As this Lord knew, if he could serve someone who was difficult to serve, it was not this limited action that would change or help this person, but the life from heaven that would descend within that relationship. As a result of this miracle that person would be able to realize that he had to change his or her life. So indeed, our Lord's goal was to teach us how to make the foundation for life to accompany us like it accompanied him wherever he went, since he knew if we do not have life, we cannot help or heal anyone else. Therefore, if the Shepherd, our Lord did come to create a religion, it surely is not a religion that we know today. The religions we see today have a tendency to emphasize that they are great and they demean every other religion. Since our Shepherd and Lord never did that throughout his life, the God of the universe could come so close to him, to the point that he could call God his Father.

If this path seems attractive to us, surely before we begin to relate well with others, we have to know what others represent for us. If we can truly value others, then we can make relationships through which life is created and we will receive the blessing of God's love accordingly. If we do this over and over, the program of destruction will be removed from our minds and at the same time we will be cleansed from the elements of death that are scattered throughout our bodies.

In conclusion we can say, the lesson of our Shepherd and Lord Jesus was to value what he valued, to recognize what he recognized, and to learn to relate with what he related with. If we do so, then life will be with us and we will become persons who are considered to be beautiful. Until that day our original destiny is waiting to be fulfilled, like the creation is waiting for us to realize our destiny ever since the day human beings lost their destiny, portrayed in the Scriptures as, "The creation waits in eager expectation for the sons of God to be revealed" (Rom. 8:19).

If we want to give hope to the creation, we will not continue to just wait, but we will begin to fulfill what we have not achieved so far. The more we make effort to see duality, the more we will become persons who carry the same thought as the Lord. And the more we practice duality, the more our flesh will become sanctified, the same as our Lord's flesh was sanctified. If we can fulfill all these things, we will become like jars filled with the water of life and therefore we will also be able to nourish others.

As he said, it will be done.

Choose Wisely Your Idol

 There was a time when a little boy and a little girl were gazing up every day at the window in their home. The reason they looked up at the window was because they were too small for their little eyes to see over the window ledge. Actually, they felt themselves quite inferior to that window. Yet after a couple of birthdays, the little boy and girl realized that maybe it was time they could finally see through that window. Still, to do so, they needed to find some boxes and pillows to put beneath their feet, in order to see at last what the window had to show to them. Therefore, one day when their mother was busy in another room, they looked at each other and ran quickly to a cabinet under the stairs where they had seen some wooden boxes. They carried the boxes to a spot below this intriguing window, with its bright yellow frame, and then they lifted the curtain that protected the window glass so they could see better what was there.

When the children's eyes arrived at the level of the glass, they were able to distinguish something through it. In that moment, they discovered that the window was something that permitted them to see through to what was outside, and indeed they realized what was outside the house was absolutely different from what was inside the house.

So due to this happy discovery, the children were standing with their noses stuck to the window, while their eyes were traveling all over the horizon. They realized there was a little road that passed almost in front of the house, and on either side there was green grass that looked like it would be nice for their feet to walk upon.

In that moment when their eyes were moving from left to right, and up and down, many little thoughts came to them, as if the pages of a picture book were turning in front of them.

But suddenly they heard some sounds coming from the kitchen and they knew who it could be. Quickly they moved their little feet down from the boxes to the floor, and hurried to put the wooden boxes back where they found them under the stairway. Then they returned to their respective places so their mother would not recognize anything unusual about them and especially so she would not ask them questions, because they did not want anybody to know what they had discovered.

But regardless how obedient they were about staying in the house, they realized their minds were constantly thinking about what they had seen through the window on that special day.

Now, who knows how many days passed after their discovery of what was on the other side of the window, but whatever they saw that day seemed like a dream or a vision, showing them there was something different from what they knew at home. Then one day, they found the door of their house standing open, seeming to beckon them to come outside.

Therefore they decided that was the moment to put their feet on the doorstep of the house, and they started to move their little feet without really knowing where they wanted to go. Soon they found they were getting closer to the road they had seen from the window, and in the moment their feet stepped onto that dusty little road, all the ideas they had when they were looking through the window came back to them, but this time they found themselves living the dream.

They were so proud to see their ideas coming true! As they walked along the dusty road, they remembered the idea they had to run and play in the little meadow, and now this idea was inviting them to venture inside the green land in front of them. Therefore, they decided to accept that proposition and to approach a place they had never known. So, together, the little boy and the little girl and their idea felt they were one, and their joy carried them along, until the moment they met a long dark fence.

As they turned their faces to look up at this severe fence, suddenly their feet came to a halt. I do believe it was the dark color that made them stop. But in spite of the sturdy bars and upright posts that stood just a few feet away, the place where the children's eyes were looking was between the bars, where they could see the waving, green grass stretching on beyond, and this green color seemed to be asking them to forget the black that presented an obstacle and to come to visit it.

Regardless of the friendliness of the grass' appearance, as they moved closer to the fence, they could hear the fence telling them, "Children, it is absolutely forbidden to pass," but when they focused on the grass, they heard the grass saying, "It would be so nice if you could visit me and walk on top of me." So notwithstanding the command of the fence, the invitation of the grass bid them accept its adventurous call, and therefore they decided to pass their little bodies between those wooden bars to see what the grass had to offer to them. When they had scrambled through the fence and were standing with their feet on the other side, they saw only the grass, and they literally forgot the fence's message.

So because the children had only one focus in their minds, which was this meadow of grass, they felt an immense sense of freedom, almost like flying. Their legs seemed to become longer and to lift them upward, and they began to run and leap like deer when they smell the new grass after a sudden rain, frolicking any place they like with the sense that all the land is theirs to enjoy.

This meadow, which may have seemed small from an adult scale, still looked immense to the eyes of the little children. And there among the tall grass that came almost to their heads, they were leaping for joy, to the left and to the right, in a disorganized way that looked quite different from the way they were taught to walk by their mother.

But regardless of their irregular movements, the little boy and little girl were advancing through the meadow. Maybe it was their gestures that directed them where to go, or maybe it was their eyes that were driving their feet. As they went, their voices filled the air with squeaks and shouts, as they called to each other with tones of excitement, "Do you see this? Do you see what I see?"

Suddenly their pace slowed down because some bright colors caught their eyes. As they approached more closely, they realized it was a little group of flowers, seeming lonely to their eyes. And later, when they remembered this part, the children thought the flowers must have been lonely because no one had dared to pass over the fence to look at them, and they must have been happy to see someone who would not eat them but would just enjoy to see them. So the little children, who were not so tall anyway, bent their knees to see the clusters of bright flowers more closely, and they discovered to their surprise that while the petals were blue like the sky, the center of each flower was yellow. And just to look at these bright blossoms made them feel like they had discovered a new kind of flower that no one ever saw before.

The fingers of the children began moving, as if pushed by some magic power, and they reached right through the blue petals to the little yellow centers. And the moment they touched the centers, they felt their fingers and their hands starting to change color, becoming yellow and blue like the flowers, and eventually their arms and their faces also! And then the children looked at each other and laughed, saying, "Look at your yellowy face! Did you see what happened to you? Did you see your bluey arms?"

"No, it's you, not me!"

Then they laughed to the point their joy compressed into tears that flowed from their eyes. They laughed until they fell over, flat on the grass that cushioned them and bent over them caringly.

Then after a moment the children stood up and look around, turning their eyes to the left and to the right. And according to the direction of their heads and their bodies, they began again to run this way and that way through the meadow until they saw a tall, red flower standing alone.

Because this flower was tall enough to look them in the face, they went very close to see inside her petals, and then they found their miniature noses had become red with pollen. What was amazing about this flower, which looked so proud to be red, was that she seemed shocked that someone could dare to steal her pollen, and the children suddenly stepped back because they could hear her saying, "Who can it be that is bigger than any normal creature, coming to visit me?"

Indeed, if the children could have asked why the flower was shocked, the answer would have been that their small noses were much bigger than the friendly honeybees that traditionally came to visit her. But after recovering from her shock, the flower realized she couldn't run or fly away from them, and therefore she humbly accepted to be looked at and touched by the noses of the little boy and girl, who really only wanted to see her very close up with their eyes, without realizing their noses were bumping her at the same time.

As for the children, upon seeing the pollen on each other's noses, they started to move their lips into the shape of a quarter moon, to the point that their eyes squeezed with joy until it overwhelmed them, making them forget that there were some who would soon come looking for them with worried eyes, furrowed foreheads and waving arms, and who were at that very moment gathering information all around the village that would lead them to find the children. But for the children and their adventure, the feeling of joy went to their heads and made them forget where they came from.

Looking around suddenly, the children noticed a large rock in the middle of the field, and the impressiveness of that rock made them decide to place their feet very deliberately, one in front of the other, trying to figure out how to approach it. When they arrived close to the rock, they realized it was much bigger than they were and questioned whether it was okay to climb it. They evaluated themselves from their height and the length of their legs and arms, and after looking again more carefully, they realized the rock did not look too difficult for their limbs to scale and at the same time did not appear too intimidating to their minds.

So they reached their hands above their heads, hoping their little fingers would somehow lift their little bodies up the rock, and by some miracle or special power that seemed to come from out of nowhere, their fingers found a grip to hold on to and their little feet were scrambling up. And however it happened, they found their whole bodies moving to the top of the rock.

When they arrived there, they realized their bodies felt suddenly weak and tired, therefore they chose to sit down on top of the rock. And as they sat there, they felt it was a big accomplishment to be on the summit of this rock, which based on their effort looked like a high mountain. And besides feeling happy, they felt they were huge, not because their bodies had suddenly grown at the speed of light but because the rock added some height to their perspective. So regardless the children had climbed a rock that was only several feet high, for them it seemed they were like their father when he had accomplished something, happy and victorious.

As they sat there, they began to observe their surroundings from the top of this majestic rock that dominated the landscape. They realized they could see everything clearly around the meadow as if it were close to them, and as they gazed in every direction, they tried to see the place from where they had first stepped onto the grass.

Suddenly a worry came to their heads as they recalled the famous fence that had warned them not to pass, and they stood up and squinted their eyes in hope of finding any object that would help them remember where they had come from. But their searching was in vain, and because they realized they did not know the way back, a dismal feeling came over them, while a darkness came to invade their little eyes, making it almost impossible to see what was far away.

After a little time of standing very still on the rock, they began to see some kind of end to the meadow, where it looked like the edge was marked by a row of trees. As they turned around in every direction, they could see trees everywhere surrounding the meadow at the edge, to the point they started to feel they were inside a crib, which made them remember something they used to be quite familiar with.

And because these trees were so tall and dense, the children started to feel their eyes enlarging from the many feelings rising inside of them, and suddenly they pictured that the trees, which had been anchored in the same place for many years, were about to walk toward them and grab them with their long branches.

So to protect each other, because their imagination was so strong, they reached for each other's hands and held them until the pain of their hands made them realize they were squeezing tightly. Then after helping each other to disconnect their fingers, they dared to look once more toward the far edges of the meadow, and this time their eyes realized that the trees did not move and they were still safely on top of the rock.

After this disconcerting event, they took a deep breath and decided to come down from their hilly rock, only this time they helped each other along the way. Then with their feet on the ground again they attempted to see where they had come from, and because they still did not see the fence where they had entered, they asked each other with squeaky voices which way they should go. And to choose which way, they decided to draw straws. So they picked a tall stem of grass and broke it into two parts, saying that the longer piece would be where the boy wanted to go and the shorter one would be where the girl wanted to go. The stem they picked was the shorter one, so they began to walk in the direction chosen by the girl, hoping that someone invisible would lead them back to the dark-colored railings of the fence.

But after walking many steps they still could not perceive where the fence was, and they started to feel worried that they had become lost through their adventure. But still they continued to move their little legs and to hurry through the tall grass, until the fear that clouded their minds began to evaporate like a fog in the morning, and because it was more clear around them, suddenly their attention came around to a small object.

This object was red with many little spots, and due to the fact they did not really know what it was, they considered that it was a huge ladybug sitting there in front of them. As they gazed at this huge ladybug, they remembered that they had heard a story that ladybugs bring good luck to those who find them. And because of this thought, they no longer felt lost but instead rather secure.

But when the little boy brought his face closer to the ladybug, he saw that she did not seem afraid of him, in fact she did not seem to have any eyes to see him. Then they realized it was not a ladybug at all, but it was maybe something else, something dangerous. As this thought passed through their heads, their faces transformed again from joy to caution; but still curious, they moved closer and closer to this intricate non-ladybug, and all the while, they were discussing about what else it could be.

When they realized it did not have legs or any other way of moving, they remembered that one time their father had warned them about something they might find in the woods that looked attractive like a ladybug but was dangerous like a wolf. But still to the eyes of the little children, this colorful object looked beautiful, so they reached toward it with their hands until they heard inside their little heads, "Do not touch! Do not touch!" In that moment, their hands stopped a few inches from the object, and the question came again, 'What can this colorful object be, in the middle of the meadow, which looks so attractive but cannot be touched?'

So after circling around this intriguing form they had never seen before and thinking about their father, they began to remember that he had spoken once about some plants growing in the woods, some of which are good for eating, but others which should absolutely not be touched, but only admired for their beauty. And in that moment they realized the object in front of them was a mushroom and, regardless of its beauty, it could be the one they should be careful about. So although they did not know what kind of mushroom it was, they began to experience many real emotions inside of them and, based on what they felt, they realized this mushroom could be dangerous to them.

After quickly stepping away from the ladybug that became a dangerous mushroom, their emotion started to subside to the point they could regain the ability to think, and again their thoughts turned toward the famous fence that had told them to not pass. But regardless their desire was topmost in their heads, their legs started to feel very tired, so they decided to slow down their steps.

Indeed, if we could have seen the children in this specific moment, we would have noticed that their expressions showed they had been through something, which surely we can believe they had. So after all these experiences, they decided to sit down in the grass, which looked ready to receive them. The grass where they sat appeared blue green and yellow green, and indeed when their eyes came close they saw many different kinds of grass. And regardless of their lack of knowing the different kinds of grass, they felt super joyful to be in the middle of this sea of grass that reached almost to their heads when they were sitting there.

So after resting in this place for what was maybe only a few minutes, they heard a sound from somewhere far away. They tried to hide behind the grass and make their bodies smaller than they already were, small enough to be invisible, but they could still hear the sounds. And because the sounds were not clear enough for them to perceive what they were, the children started to imagine that some large animals were maybe coming close to them, and from this thought a feeling of terror started to cover them.

Then the little boy, as brave as he was big, told his little sister, "Don't worry, I will protect you with all my three feet of courage." Nevertheless, the two of them continued to crouch where they were, hoping the tall grass would bend over to cover them from view. But while their eyes could see nothing but the grass all around them, actually their bodies were visible from afar, especially for some who knew the land.

And suddenly the noises they were hearing sounded familiar, like voices they had heard before, and they started to recognize their names being called out. The little boy and girl looked at each other, and one part of them felt so happy that someone knew their names, and another part of them so sad because their adventure would soon be ended. So for a short time they wondered in their heads whether they should hide a little longer, hoping the land would sink a bit beneath them so they could be more invisible, or if they should stand up and show their little bodies and admit they were safe -- not swallowed by anything, like they wanted the grass to do, and not poisoned by a mushroom. And through the moments of waiting to see who it was that had discovered them, they were remembering the rock that told them they could be as strong as their father, and the trees that had actually never walked over to grab them, and the flowers that had made them change colors. All these memories were ringing inside their heads like bells ringing in the steeple of the village church.

After all these mixed feelings, they decided to reconcile with the ones who were calling their names, so they got up and walked slowly toward the voices until that dark fence came into view. Soon they could distinguish someone tall standing behind the fence, and as they approached, this person reached to them with big, strong hands to lift them over the bars and up onto his shoulders. From this height, they could see in the distance a group of people running towards them, looking so happy, waving and cheering like they were victorious.

So regardless it looks like this story could end here, in later years, the children who were all grown up still told of how all the people came running toward them, passing them from one person to the next with their strong hands, lifting them up into the sky like they were the most victorious little children. They remembered how their father and mother and all the village people were crowding around, wanting to touch and cherish them, some of them trying to kiss them as if they were flowers, and indeed they did feel as if they were flowers. More and more kisses were coming to them, and some people patted them and some thumped them hard, some of them squeezed and some held onto their little hands. To the children, it seemed as if their joy would never end, and regardless they did not laugh out loud, the desire was inside them.

They remembered that after being cherished by all the villagers, they came back to the arms of their father and mother, and suddenly their little bodies went down to a normal height and they could feel the road under their feet as they started to walk side by side with all these people who looked so happy and relieved. After several steps, they saw their house in front of them and realized it was the home where they were born and where they had always lived, so they entered through the doorway, and the people who had rejoiced to find them began to depart for their own homes.

Then the children were alone with their parents, and they found themselves breathing a big sigh of relief, which came as a shock, without knowing how it was possible. And after a short time at home they started to rediscover what belonged to them and to play with their toys again.

The Origin of our Feelings

So, what can be the lesson inside this little story? When we look carefully at what was written, we can see that according to each thing the children saw, touched and imagined, they felt different emotions arising in them. That is the reason we can say their adventure – besides being physical and mental -- was surely an emotional adventure as well. In this story, we can see several dimensions intertwined with each other, like the way the children's mental perception mingled with the reality of the physical events and the mysterious dimension of all of their senses and feelings.

For example, when the children saw the clusters of blue and yellow flowers, the flowers they saw were real and the colors were also real. But we can ask, did these flowers have the power to transfer their color to the children, or was it the joy of the children that colored their perception? As we recall, the children perceived their arms and faces as becoming the same color as the flowers' petals and centers.

It was actually their joy over the flowers that made them feel their bodies were also becoming yellow and blue.

Similarly, when they stood on top of the rock, they created a specific thought by choosing their father as a reference, and in that moment they felt they were strong like him. This positive thought re-created in them the sense of security that they had when they were with their father.

But when the children directed their eyes to the edge of the field with its border of trees, they created an imaginary thought about what the trees could do to them, like walking toward them and grabbing them with their long branches. This grandiose negative imagination also created a multitude of feelings in them, this time on the side of fear.

From the story of the children, we can observe the process of how feelings are created. We can see that when the children looked at a physical object and had a specific thought in their minds connected to that object, a circuit was created that permitted them to receive a specific emotion. For example, when they looked at the trees and connected the trees to thoughts of aggression, those thoughts formed a relationship that automatically produced a feeling of fearfulness. And when the little children saw something red with black spots, at first they were happy because they believed it was a ladybug, which they associated with joyful thoughts. But when they identified the object as a dangerous toadstool, pessimistic thoughts started to come, which caused a different feeling to pass through their flesh.

By observing each event in the story of the little children, we can see that in order to produce a feeling, first we need to be aware of an object that is in front of us, either physically or in our mind, and from that stage we need to associate the object with a word or group of words that is strong enough to create a pole, either positive or negative. And then according to the way we choose to compose our thought, we will receive a feeling, which can be viewed as the fruit of the thought and the physical matter.

Through this observation, we can realize that we as humans have the power to dismantle any feeling, if we are observant of the thoughts inside our mind in the moment we choose an object. As well, we as humans can re-create a feeling we once had if we are able to retrieve the thought connected to a physical event that caused that feeling, which many times is stored inside our mind like an archive of photos. But it would indeed be difficult to have a feeling if there were no thought in the first place connected to what we see, and due to this we would not be able to feel the multitude of emotions that we humans usually consider to be such an important part of life, such as excitement, suspense, drama and joy.

If we look at the many stories that people like to write or read, we might say that feelings are living within the thoughts we construct when we observe a situation -- or maybe feelings live between the thoughts and the objects we observe. But regardless of how our feelings begin and where they exist, we need to ask ourselves what category of feelings we wish to experience. Depending of the specific category of feelings we choose, like positive or negative, or joyfulness or drama or a mixture of both, we will need to remember to use the category of thought that will create or maintain the corresponding feelings we wish to have, for a short time, or for the duration of our life.

The Connection between Thought and Feeling

If you look back to the story of the children, who after all were very young, it looks like they did not choose their thoughts with a very high consciousness or awareness; instead, all kinds of thoughts were coming to them in connection with the objects they perceived or believed they saw. Because of the unstructured imagination that circulated inside their heads, a multitude of feelings was unfolding inside of them according to their perceptions. And due to that, we can consider that they went through an emotional adventure, which all began with a physical adventure that was amplified by their thoughts.

If we believe that an adult is much more in control of his thoughts than a child, then he should be able to distinguish between what he wants to feel and not feel. Therefore we can identify an adult human being as one who has the pleasure of choosing a specific thought that has the power to liberate a specific feeling, according to what he so much wants to feel again and again. Similarly, an adult human being also has the capacity to dismiss a specific thought, in connection to a physical object, if he does not want to experience the feeling that this thought will give to him.

From this standpoint we can see that an adult human being has immense power over himself, because he can choose what he wants to think anytime, anywhere. As well, we can understand why an adult human being feels the honor and responsibility to protect a child from anyone who tries to create a thought in the mind of that child, because he knows the young one cannot control very well the thoughts he will choose in connection with what he sees, touches and hears.

Therefore, based on a child's incapacity to dismantle a thought from a secular event in order to not feel what he does not want to feel, we refer to a child as being vulnerable to the world of thought because he does not know yet the relationship between the things he perceives or touches and the thoughts he can choose in connection with them. He surely also does not know what kind of energy may be released from this relationship between thought and object and subsequently what energy can be manifested in his body, since every emotion created carries a certain quantity and quality of energy with it. While a child has this vulnerable aspect, we as adult beings have the honor of knowing the secret of the relationship between the thought and the object and the feeling that comes as a result. This is the reason many people will devote themselves to the field of mastering a thought, in order to be able to create emotion in the people around them.

If you read again the story of the little children and revisit the moments when they saw the flowers, the mushroom, the rock, and the trees, you can observe what kind of thoughts came to them in each individual moment. Additionally, you can guess that they must have acquired their knowledge of these objects from someone who had already experienced them. So based on seeing what a young mind is capable of, we should not underestimate the quantity of thoughts human beings can absorb during their youth, thoughts that naturally will be used when they encounter physical objects and situations around them later in life, and which will automatically create feelings in different categories. And because the youthful education that each person receives is different from every other person, this explains why some children will cry and others will laugh at the same event.

Therefore we can understand that when the children in this story found an object like the rock or the trees, they associated with that object a specific thought that had been dormant in their mind. For example, when they approached the rock and succeeded in reaching the top, they suddenly remembered their father and compared their achievement to the exclamation they heard their father make when he achieved something, and therefore they felt strong like him.

In general, everything around our life has the capacity to remind us of specific thoughts that we learned previously from some source, and if we observe what category these thoughts belong to, it will be to either the category of optimism or the category of pessimism. Therefore, the same object can make us feel good or bad, depending on the thought we associate with it. If we look back at the adventure of the children, we will realize that as they were walking from place to place, they saw different objects and identified them as something familiar, based on the family they came from and the kind of instruction they had already received.

If we could go around and interview different children about their individual experiences, we would see how the thought that one child chooses when he sees, touches or imagines an object will be very different from the thought of another child, regardless their external environment may look the same. How is it possible that children can have different emotional experiences, even though the objects they see and touch are the same? Of course, we can try to look inside a human being's feeling to know what different emotions he feels, but this will not reveal the process by which the feeling was created, because the only way to know the origin of the feeling will be if we can record what thought was in a person's mind in the moment before he experienced the feeling.

Each Person's Education is Unique

Regardless many people can experience the same physical occurrence, the thought that each person has in that moment is different from the next person. Usually our ability to produce and manipulate ideas makes us identify ourselves as smart, unique and, especially, creative. But although we usually value thoughts, an enormous quantity of thoughts can also make us feel complex and eventually confused.

One thing is sure, regardless we may all perform similar actions, touch similar objects or experience similar physical events, we are far from having the same thoughts. In fact, our composition of ideas in connection to the reality we experience can be so different between one person and another that it is very possible to misunderstand each other, and the resultant feelings can even cause us to depart from each other. For this reason we surely can understand why it is so complex for human beings to relate with each other.

To illustrate this point, when the children in the story ventured inside the meadow, we can recognize that their minds produced a different thought according to each object they observed, like the mushroom or the red flowers, according to their education, and each thought belonged, knowingly or unknowingly, to the category of either pessimism or optimism. Likewise, if we have learned some thoughts belonging to the category of optimism, which can originate from a poem, for instance, or our mother's favorite saying, we will often apply these thoughts when we perceive a specific object or when we imagine an event or perform our work.

On the other hand, if our minds were educated with thoughts from the category of pessimism, we will naturally use these thoughts and connect them to everything we encounter. After applying these pessimistic thoughts in our daily life over many years, this habitual work of our mind will settle into a character of negativity, due to the quantity of pessimistic feelings we produced throughout our life.

To return to the story, if you were permitting yourself to walk with the children through their adventure, you also must have had many thoughts coming to your mind in connection to what the children saw. Although you may not have noticed your thoughts because you were focusing on the story, you surely must have also experienced a multitude of feelings inside yourself, moving from up to down, from left to right, and front to back, just as the children also experienced many feelings

So regardless the story was written about the adventure of the children, we can also observe that in the midst of reading about this adventure, what the children imagined in connection to what they saw also caused us to create some thoughts, regardless that what was real became unreal and what was imaginary became real in the children's minds. And regardless whether they chose a conventional way to explain a real event or used a misperception toward an object they saw, many feelings were still capable of inflating inside of them, as well as in us, according to our thoughts. Indeed we would be obliged to agree that everything they said was true, not because what they thought was correct, but because their thoughts were capable of making us feel something.

For example, when the children were approaching the ladybug that actually was not a ladybug, they connected it with the thought of good luck, and this thought permitted them to have a joyful feeling. However, when the children realized it was not a ladybug but actually a dangerous mushroom, their thoughts changed drastically, and their feelings turned into fear where before their feelings had been joy and hope.

Likewise, if we as adults have cultivated our intellect over the years, we also will have a chance to recall the knowledge or viewpoint we have learned and use it toward anything our eyes perceive or our hands may touch. In the moment we use a thought toward an object, we will receive a feeling, positive or negative. In our current time, many human beings feel the necessity to learn a wide variety of thoughts for the sake of being intelligent and cultivated. As well, they tend to have the desire to be close to every kind of person and to understand everyone's feelings. They therefore listen to a multitude of both pessimistic and optimistic thoughts in order to relate with others, often without being careful about where the thoughts they are listening to might lead them. And the reason human beings in our current time pursue the dream of understanding other people is, I believe, for the purpose of being considered cosmopolitan in their outlook or diplomatic in their behavior.

One thing is sure, by acquiring many categories of thought, we gain an immense ability to actually change our thoughts at the speed of light, based on what we see or even based on our misperceptions. As a result, we juggle with all kinds of moods within ourselves and through this process characterize ourselves as emotional and changeable beings, even concluding that our feelings are out of our control.

The Source of Our Thoughts

You may question, same as I, where our thoughts come from—what is the source of all the thoughts we receive in the moment we look at something? Do thoughts come from our mind that was educated, or do thoughts arise from the object in the moment we see it? Or, we can say, do the thoughts jump out from the object and come to us or do the thoughts jump out from our brain to the object?

If our minds had received no education at all about a specific object, then when we looked at this object we might expect to see it just as it is, without connecting it to any thought from our mental file. This would demonstrate that the material objects around us have neutral characteristics, without the capacity to tell us what they wish us to think about them. Therefore, if many people could observe the same object without preconceptions, they would enjoy the discovery that they could all view this object in the same way. But maybe having an identical viewpoint would not attract anyone because they feel they would be categorized as simplistic or unimaginative, qualities which in our time do not appear ambitious or appealing.

If the children in the story had no specific education in their heads, they would not have had any pre-conceived thoughts connected to the objects they saw, although they would still have enjoyed each object in all its complexity of form, function, color and purpose. But usually because we are already educated with certain thoughts, it is almost inevitable that some thought comes every time we are in front of a physical object, and as a result the thought becomes the most important part of our experience, more so than what we are actually seeing. In fact, because they were children and therefore relatively uneducated and inexperienced, they could view many of the objects in a pure and unbiased fashion, and let their imaginations run away with them, like their thought that the trees could walk.

Therefore a question arises: is it possible to feel joy from an object without our having a specific thought that can transform what we see, either blocking our experience or creating turmoil? In other words, can we enjoy just looking at objects and observing them as they are? Do human beings absolutely need a pre-conceived thought when they observe an object, in order to feel something?

Indeed, if we are looking at an object without any thought in our mind, we will realize that our eyes are more observant and more sensitive to the object. But it is also true that if we have an optimistic, or grateful, thought toward the object we are seeing and observing, we will experience a higher level of joy as a result than if we did not add this thought. So if someone chooses the best thought toward a specific object, a thought that has the potential to generate a positive feeling, then this person will have the highest qualification to enjoy everything existing around him. But if a person is educated with pessimistic thoughts and applies them to what he sees and touches, the feelings produced will resemble despair and fearfulness.

If we look again at the children in the story, it seems clear that the children indeed had an adventure, while at the same time, if we compare them with adult beings, it looks like we adults also like to create an adventure every day, especially an emotional adventure, which we often achieve by reading books or watching television. So we can remark that the reason many of us, like the children, enjoy finding within our imagination or memory a multitude of different thoughts is for the purpose of creating a multitude of feelings within ourselves. This means we are occupied throughout the day with creating an intellectual adventure in order to have an emotional adventure that will cause us to feel of happiness, joy, tension, guilt or depression.

Can We Choose our Thoughts?

If a human chooses to experience a spectrum of feelings on a daily basis, he will first need to choose a spectrum of thoughts with the potential to create many different feelings. But if a human wants to be joyful every day, he needs to choose only those thoughts that will permit him to feel joy, happiness and peace. Likewise if someone is always tense or depressed, it means this person has cultivated loyalty toward pessimistic thoughts, which cause him to sink under their weight on a daily basis.

We can also question, do we human beings carry a tendency toward one specific category of feeling from our birth, without the potential to choose what we want to feel? Or are we responsible for the thoughts we choose, which result in making us fearful or joyful, depressed or impressed? Indeed, if we analyze the story of the little children one more time, at certain points they chose a thought in connection to what they were seeing, such as something they heard their parents say or what was read to them from their little books.

When we observe adult beings, we can see that they can live an adventure during their daily lives that looks similar to what the children experienced. But contrary to the children's experience, it is quite possible that adult beings will not maintain the freedom to choose their adventure once they begin to settle themselves into a certain pattern of thought. Instead, due to this settlement they can arrive at a stage where they are obliged to use the same thought again and again, which will cause them to experience the same feeling again and again.

For example, if a person were educated to be pessimistic, he would eventually achieve a stable state of depression and many related feelings in the same category. If that person wished to change the pattern of negativity that he had achieved, perhaps because he found in himself a desire for optimism, he would need to embark upon a journey that would permit him eventually to achieve an optimistic thought every time he saw something, regardless of the difficulty to do so. Because this person had maintained negativity for many years, it would demand from him an extra effort over a substantial period of time before he could arrive to the place where optimistic thoughts could dwell securely in the framework of his mind.

Therefore, based on this reality, which many times has hurt or limited us, if we as human beings do not examine the nature of all the thoughts we are using, we can easily progress from a pessimistic thought to a negative thought and finally to a depressing thought, without realizing where we are going until we reach the end of that adventure, which looks more like a nightmare. And although we might distantly remember some feelings like joy or happiness, even if we wished to re-create those emotions, we would be almost incapable of changing our direction. We would no longer know the way to regain the experience of joyfulness and happiness, until a time when we would be so tired of our suffering that we would consider it a priority to focus our mind on thoughts that would create a positive emotional adventure.

Based on knowing the power of emotion, we can say that a human being who allows himself to have a specific category of thought for a long period of time will start to believe these thoughts were with him all his life. And if he is well trained, to the point he can no longer cut off from a specific feeling like tension or depression, it means this person is united perfectly with certain thoughts. His experience will make him believe he cannot change, and eventually he will come to the conclusion that he is a prisoner of his thoughts or he will believe this is his character.

In the process of our education, there are many kinds of thoughts we are presented with. However, these thoughts are useless until we make the conscious effort to choose and believe them. From the moment we consciously choose them, these thoughts, which are connected to matter, will release their emotional contents inside us, to the point that our bodies will exhibit the character and form of this emotion.

We can see that many human beings are adventurous and love the variety of different thoughts. For the sake of adventure, they have a tendency to choose thoughts that can make them discover some kind of extreme feeling, like ecstasy or terror. And then, without being aware of the direction they are taking, their adventure can turn out to be not a positive adventure but a trap or a prison, if they don't know how to come back from it. This kind of adventure is especially dangerous if a person chooses thoughts from the realm of pessimism. On the other hand, if you believe in words of optimism, you will be able to experience a multitude of feelings of happiness, which will characterize you as a positive person and distinguish you from those who are negative.

The Power of the Realm of Thought

Through these observations we can start to fathom the power of the realm of thought and to understand the mysterious mechanisms we are built with. Indeed, we cannot ignore the words we believe in, because words were created to express the mental side of what we observe in the physical realm. Every time we recall an event, or try to describe an event to someone, we will discover that the thoughts we initially had during that event are still printed in our memory and can re-surface in the moment we are explaining the event, to the point all the feelings we experienced can come back again, fresh and alive, as if we were reliving the situation.

If a certain event was not a pleasant one and we retain the thought we had about it, each time we recall that event we will be obliged to experience the unpleasant feeling over and over. This will occur until we choose a different thought, or until someone outside us helps us to change the thought. In the moment the thought that was printed in us is completely removed, we will no longer feel what we used to feel, even though the memory of the event can still be there.

Therefore, knowing the power of thought, we can understand that whatever experience we have, the core of our adventure is created by the thoughts we have in the process of that adventure. For example, let us observe ourselves when we are reading a novel. If the book vividly describes both the physical events of the story and the thoughts of the characters, we as the reader will feel many emotions, to the point that what we experience through the book can seem more real than what we experience in our daily life. And if the feelings the writer invokes in us are feelings we like and we want to experience, we will consider the writer to be a great author and a skillful storyteller.

Now, if we also wish to become great storytellers and champions of communicating our feelings to others, the first thing we will need to do is to give a detailed description of the physical events that occurred, and the next thing will be to explain the thoughts we had in the midst of those events. If we can clearly communicate these two major categories, the person who is listening will be able to feel what we felt and will recognize us as expressive persons. But on the other hand, if we cannot vividly describe the situation and the thoughts that accompanied it, we will be incapable of making anyone feel what we felt.

Similarly, to achieve the realm of feeling in our own selves, the first part is to educate our minds to be able to remember thoughts. Eventually, we will realize that the thoughts we have trained ourselves to remember are deeply embedded inside our mind, whether they belong to the category of pessimism or optimism. Then, regardless what external situations occur around us and what objects we see, the dormant thoughts in our mind will always come back to us and will make us feel something.

For example, if you love your parents very much, it means you have been educated to use certain positive thoughts towards your parents. It is this consistent pattern of keeping positive thoughts toward your parents that permits you to have feelings of love for them. With this base, if you see a stately tree in the park and think the tree is standing strong like your parents, this optimistic thought in connection to your parents will enable you to experience love for them one more time, as well as amplifying your appreciation of the tree. The same will be true of any object you use as a symbol of your parents' love.

You can use this method to feel love in any circumstance. Then, even if someone you love is no longer with you physically, if you can continue to use a loving thought that corresponds to him or her, you will still be able to feel love. And by maintaining loving thoughts securely in your mind every day and connecting them with anything and anyone you see, those thoughts will permeate you to the point that the inevitable result will be feelings of happiness, joy and peace.

If I could ask any adult human being one question, it would be, "What do you want to feel?" If people choose the desire to feel happy, for example, then to achieve that result they will first need to find a specific thought that has the ability to release the feeling inside of them called 'happiness'. Similarly, if they choose to want to feel tension, they will need to receive an education in pessimistic thoughts in order to be able to experience the feeling of stress or pressure.

So, based on knowing that our emotions are the result of thoughts, if we wish to be people of joy, we will need to research which thoughts will permit us to feel joy. And if we want to experience a wide range of feelings, like depression, excitement, despair, joy and boredom, we will need to explore many categories of thought in order to create this multitude of feelings.

However, if we wish to maintain a certain type of feeling, we will need to develop loyalty toward the specific category of thought required. Unless we maintain that loyalty, it is understandable that our feelings will not be able to settle into one specific category but instead will always be vacillating.

From this viewpoint, if human beings want to arrive at a place where joy and love for one another are stable inside themselves, they must have the characteristic of extreme loyalty toward certain thoughts, in order to experience the same feelings over and over toward the people they want to love. Certainly, to be able to constantly extract the same feeling of love by choosing a specific thought shows that a person has an immense internal quality of loyalty.

Our Thought is Our Idol

Looking now from a different perspective, I will say that the reason we can be loyal to whatever thought we choose and regard as our own is because we consider that thought to be great — so great that it can be viewed as our private 'idol', based on the value and high respect we give to it. Because we have an attitude of loyalty toward this thought, we do not want to disgrace it or offend it, and therefore it is acceptable to believe that the thought we hold supreme is actually an idol.

Indeed, if a thought were just a passing idea to be used to express something, then a thought should be called only a thought. But in the moment a person will dedicate his life for this thought or accept to lose his life to defend it, then the thought has to be elevated to the position of an internal idol. So although this word 'idol' does not seem to fit with our view of the 21st century, we indeed can develop a lifetime oath toward the thought we value, the same as people have done towards idols made of gold or stone or wood.

If we look at historical times when human beings pledged to be faithful to their idols, it was not just for the purpose of believing in something, but it was because people had discovered that they received specific feelings when they expressed belief in those idols, and they wished to receive over and over again those same feelings. Similar to these old traditions of idol worship, we can say the main reason human beings try to choose a thought as their idol is to become one with it, because as we now know, it is by embracing a thought that we gain a feeling.

If the idol or the thought we choose is composed, for example, of words of pessimism and we unite with this thought many times in our daily life, we will receive the feeling of depression as payment for our dedication to this idol. Perhaps for some reason we unconsciously want to feel depressed and have learned to like the feeling of depression. However, this feeling did not arrive in us by accident, but it came because we developed the characteristic of enduring loyalty toward a thought that had a negative core, regardless we believed it to be a good thought. Based on our loyalty, this idol will endow us with its specific energy, which over time will have a noticeable effect on our flesh, namely, we will begin to look heavy and dry.

Likewise, if we choose an idol constructed of words expressing optimism, the properties of this idol will only begin to be perceived when we have affirmed our loyalty to it many times. Through this daily effort, we will place ourselves in a position to receive its properties, which can be peace and joy, calmness and serenity. However, unless we choose deliberately and consciously to return many times to this idol, we will forfeit the privilege of receiving the feelings that this idol bestows.

Now we can conclude, if we as adult beings choose an idol that contains the nature of depression, we only can feel depressed. And if the idol is composed of negativity, we will receive and generate anger. If the idol is made with words of an embracing and welcoming nature, we will find peace in ourselves. If the idol has humorous words, we will receive buoyancy and good will, and so on.

Interestingly, if we have the desire to experience a multitude of feelings in different categories, we will need to share our loyalty between many different idols. This means we will need to believe that all idols are equally good, and therefore choose one of them for a short time, and then abandon it and choose another one for awhile. The good point of experimenting with many idols is that we can discover the taste of each idol or thought and can become a person with a multitude of feelings, which I think demands a lot of knowledge and hard work, especially on the part of our memory, because it needs to remember so many words. Surely we will develop a character that is cosmopolitan in scope, due to the multitude of feelings we have experienced, although we will also become persons of limited loyalty by changing our thought often and believing all kinds of words.

An interesting aspect of this cosmopolitan character is that we will have no difficulty being approached by people who themselves carry a specific idol. This capability to see every belief as okay will make it easy for us to welcome any person who wishes to express his feelings or thoughts. We can be sure that after meeting with us, such a person will appear very happy because he will realize we understood his feelings and therefore will feel he can relate with us since we did not reject his idol or thought. Therefore he will consider us to be understanding and approachable.

But if we do not like to be so changeable and instead desire to achieve a specific feeling and maintain it throughout our life, we must first find a thought to which we will show extreme faithfulness and loyalty. If, for instance, the feelings we want to experience consistently are joy, peace and love, we need to find the special category of thought that will enable us to attain these feelings, when we have learned to maintain faith and loyalty toward that thought.

The Person Who was Loyal to the Highest Thought

If there is a person who could achieve the goal of carrying the feelings of joy, peace and love, it means that person must have understood the connection between thought and feeling.

And if there is someone who chose to use a thought that could make him attain the nature of peacefulness and loveliness, such a person must have understood the psychology of words and feelings and the power of words concerning the physical things we live with.

When we look at which person through all of history was able to achieve within himself this quality of love and peace, I have to acknowledge the person of Jesus Christ, whom I will refer to here as Doctor Jesus, because of the high quality of thought he achieved.

I do think that the reason the esteemed Dr. Jesus tried to teach humanity his thought was not just because he wanted someone to agree with him. Instead, he understood that for an adult being to attain the qualities of peace and joy, this person would need a group of thoughts that are capable of releasing the level of energy necessary to create these feelings. And these feelings would have to be created to a degree sufficient for them to dwell inside the person constantly. Therefore, it is normal that if Dr. Jesus did achieve this dimension of heart, he would have wanted to tell the people of this Earth about his thought, or his 'idol', for the purpose of empowering them to understand him, to feel what he felt, and to live how he lived.

We can realize when we look at the person of Dr. Jesus, that he must have chosen his idol firmly and loyally from a very young age, in order to be able to achieve such a peaceful personality that he could speak words like,

"Love your enemies" (Luke 6:27) as well as "Peace be with you" (John 20:19) and many other passages that we refer to him.

When we observe Dr. Jesus, it looks like he had a sense of priorities when he said, "He who believes in me will never be thirsty" (John 6:36) and "No one comes to the Father but through me" (John 14:6). The reason he wished us to believe in him was because he wanted us to adopt his idol, which had the capacity to make us feel peace, joy and eventually love, to the point that he could even say, "Anyone who loves his father or mother more than me is not worthy of me; anyone who loves his son or daughter more than me is not worthy of me" (Matt.10:35).

In other words, Dr. Jesus understood that love, peace and joy were contained within the words he was speaking, and that unless we choose them and believe in them as our idol, we will not be able to receive their properties. Therefore, we can say, the psychology Dr. Jesus used in order to help his students grow was that they should believe in his words so they would be able to receive joy, peace and love. As we accept to make more and more effort to believe in his words, this contribution puts us in a certain alignment where we can experience love for Dr. Jesus or love from him. Conversely, if we refuse to listen to his words or if we choose not to use them in our daily life, regardless we maybe know them, the effect will be that we will not receive his love, and due to this it will be impossible for us to have love for our father, mother, brother, or sister.

Based on his desire for the people to experience what he experienced, Dr. Jesus was obliged to teach a thought with the ability to release joy and peace in the ones who adhered to it. To achieve this task, he needed to find some people who wanted to believe in this idol or these words, not occasionally but with great loyalty, so that those people could carry peace and joy at the core of their being. Based on how Dr. Jesus educated himself, he must have known that his students would have to train their minds with certain thoughts for a long enough period of time for those thoughts to release sufficient energy to bring about a change in the students' personalities.

If we observe the thought or the idol of Dr. Jesus, we will perceive that the psychology he used to gain his stature must be very different from ours, because if we just read his words without intentionally wanting to believe in them, we will not be capable of feeling what he felt, since we are not using his thought as an idol. But if we can contribute by accepting to believe his words and use them in our daily life, we will begin to feel Dr. Jesus' essence. Only after we choose his thought with the sense of 'it is an idol' and accept to be loyal to it for our entire life, will we begin to know what we are capable of becoming.

Based on achieving a specific amount of energy within ourselves, we will be able to connect ourselves to Dr. Jesus through having a concentration of energy that is similar to what he has. As we practice consistently the psychology that Dr. Jesus taught, we will become so one with him that we will be capable of speaking to the people around us in the same way as he spoke in his day, even making people feel the same as he made them feel.

If we can achieve this quantity of energy within ourself, as Dr. Jesus was hoping for humans to achieve, the people around us will admire us as persons of immensely high quality based on the feelings they sense within us, and will even perceive a resemblance between our being and the nature of Dr. Jesus. And from our inner perspective, we will feel we understand Dr. Jesus and that he understands us as well. Through this intimate relationship, we will know we are one with him, which surely will make us feel secure and peaceful.

Always Choose His Thought

Perhaps we as adult beings consider that the words of Dr. Jesus are too simple, and this can be the reason we do not choose his idol and why throughout history people have revolted against his thought. But this rejection of his words is not a tragedy against Jesus but against ourselves, because it makes us unable to receive the peace and love he wanted us to feel.

Some of us perhaps did not reject Dr. Jesus' philosophy, but we may have found ourselves choosing his idol only at the times when our loneliness became more painful than we could bear. Therefore, we turned to his idol for a short time, and due to this acceptance of his words in connection to our behavior, the feeling of loneliness we were carrying was destroyed in that moment, and was replaced by a better feeling. And then, after feeling better for a certain time, we again chose to ignore his thought as useless, until the next time when the pain of loneliness became so great that we turned to him once more.

Regardless the action of turning to his thought is a momentous step, this minimal action of turning to him on only a few occasions does not have the potential to build in us the same quantity of peace and love as Dr. Jesus has. Therefore, instead of leaving his thought every time we feel better, if we as adult beings can choose consistently the thought of Dr. Jesus with the high energy it carries, we will gain from him the love that will enable us to love anyone living around us during our physical life on Earth.

After knowing what he wanted to say to us for so long, we surely can now recognize the power and the miracle of the thought of Dr. Jesus. Based on understanding how feeling is created by choosing a specific category of thought and by accepting to be as loyal to the words of Dr. Jesus as he was loyal to the One who gave the words to him, we can also become beings of love, of peace and of joy, as Dr. Jesus was a being of love, peace and joy for his Father in Heaven and the ones who could accept to recognize him.

We can now understand that Dr. Jesus wanted us to choose his idol so we could receive what he received. Through that we would be able to change and destroy the many other idols that occupy our minds. Even if we have difficulty to fully understand and accept his achievement of becoming the embodiment of love, peace and joy, and even if it is difficult for us to believe the thought that he chose as his idol, surely we can recognize that his perpetual concern was to bring human beings close to his Father in Heaven. This is the reason he always wanted to speak about his Father and love Him.

Regardless our time is different from his, if we choose his idol and use his psychology, we will find ourselves speaking about Dr. Jesus' words and loving him as well as loving his Father. And through this process of being loyal to his idol, we will surely become like Jesus or like his Father.

From now on, if you decide you want to become a loving being, you will need to find and choose the idol that will permit you to receive the love of Heaven. If you are a person who is always trying to find love, I recommend that you accept the idol of Dr. Jesus or the idol of anyone who has the same character and carries the same optimistic words as he.

From this viewpoint, we do not need to accuse ourselves for not having joy or peace or love, because now we understand that love cannot come into us unless we first pass through the process of acquiring the words that open the gate of love. Therefore, it would be advisable to observe what idols we are reading about or listening to, and begin to develop our portion of responsibility by being loyal to a divine thought, if we really want to experience love and peace and joy.

We need to realize that if we do not feel what Dr. Jesus feels for his Father and what he carries for us, it is because we did not choose his word for as long a period of time as he or with the same absoluteness. Regardless we may believe in Dr. Jesus to some degree, the fact is that if we carry depression, we obviously and even consciously must have chosen another idol or another thought that bestowed upon us the blessing of depression. And if today we as adult beings have many varying feelings, it is because we did not choose to focus on a specific idol, but instead chose all kinds of idols that created in us all kinds of feelings.

In summary, we can say that whatever feelings we experience, they are coming to us as a result of the thoughts we have been choosing for years. If we are displeased by our feelings, we should not accuse ourselves or others for what we feel but should realize that we made the wrong choice of thought. Regardless what idol we have been faithfully uniting with, it is maybe time now to adopt a thought that is guaranteed to give us what we want to feel, so that we can become the human beings we wish to be.

What is commendable about Dr. Jesus is that he felt the confidence and responsibility to explain his idol for the sake of others, hoping that we would want to take his ideology. But regardless what Dr. Jesus offered to us, we know there are many other thoughts we humans are loyal to, which originate from teachers who do not want to be held accountable for what they teach and do not give any guarantee that their thought will help us to achieve the best a human being can be. Nevertheless, we often continue to choose the idol of someone who does not take responsibility for what he or she taught, and we follow it with seriousness and loyalty to the point where we receive the feelings contained inside it, which after all do not please us. Many times we do not even check the biography or autobiography of the writer to see what kind of character his own thought produced in him. And if we accept this thought without any background references and begin to build our faith in these words, we may have difficulty admitting to ourselves the emotional result.

On the one hand, we are generally not so careful to investigate a person who advances a certain thought, especially if he comes from a prestigious university. But on the other hand, we can notice that human beings through history have been very strict and analytical when they look at the thought of Dr. Jesus, as if he were dangerous and his thought should be suspect.

In addition to analyzing the words of Dr. Jesus, people observe with intense scrutiny the ones who believe in his words, to see whether they progress according to what the critics think those people should achieve, and based on what they think Dr. Jesus preached. If they find that someone does not achieve a character up to their standard of measurement, they will feel confident to accuse the psychology of Dr. Jesus of not being the truth or to accuse that person of being a hypocrite.

In contrast to Dr. Jesus, many people who created pessimistic idols are not as well known to the public as a whole, and because of their obscurity we cannot easily research their character and the kind of life they went through, which if it were known might cause people to conclude that their thought should be viewed with caution. Indeed, many people still adopt their thought and use it loyally, without questioning whether the thought they have adopted is beneficial to their soul and heart. They will even use that thought as a curriculum for their students, who will also believe without investigating its origins, embracing it enthusiastically, until the fruit of following this unenthusiastic thought becomes manifest through them.

When we observe Dr. Jesus, we see that he did not hide his idol, but rather he wanted to promote his perfect psychology, so that we could also receive love from his Father through choosing his idol. Instead, many people felt jealous toward Dr. Jesus for the love that was perceivable in him. We may not fully know the reasons why the people of his time did not recognize what Dr. Jesus wanted to make them feel, but one thing is sure: by rejecting his teaching, those people were choosing to maintain loyalty to an idol that would make them feel despair and depression rather than the hope, joy and peace which Dr. Jesus promised they could have.

So if today we can choose the idol of Dr. Jesus by using our human talent to be loyal and faithful toward his thought, then I guarantee that the same joy he experienced will be the joy we will experience, regardless we live in a different time of history. Surely if we value his thought and believe it anew, then Dr. Jesus will not be a mysterious legend to us but he will become alive and very real in our awareness, to the point that he will see us as the real brothers and the real sisters he longs so much to have.

I hope you will choose wisely your daily idol so that you can be a person who carries peace and love in your being. And therefore, wherever you go, peace will be.

Let's us make ourselves be.

The Philosophy of We or I

𝓘f we observe what a young person does for a certain period of his evolution, it is to study the knowledge of former generations. And if we look at what category his mind is eager to be challenged in, it is in the realm of philosophy.

As a result, the study of 'philosophy' has become one of the areas that many youth encounter, and the main reason is because it contains the promise of being able to gain the wisdom of the ancients, with the hope of elevating the standard of their present lives. Therefore, based on their wish to better themselves, the students who choose to study philosophy usually feel it is meaningful to dedicate some part of their lives to this study, and they anticipate they will find some brightness in those thick and dusty volumes of the university library that will illuminate their realm of thought. Or, for the ones who are studying in recent decades, they will search through the internet for the same goal.

I believe many of you may have had the experience of wanting to research this complex subject of philosophy, perhaps because it sounded important for your quest and desire to help people. Perhaps you felt you needed to acquire the knowledge of what human beings are about in order to change what you saw around you as a young person. So, based on your discontent with the current reality of the world and your burning wish to change something, it must have seemed sensible to use your determination to study a thought that could provide the elements necessary for you to arrive, one day, at a place where you could contribute to the betterment of your society.

Because of this vision, many young souls, perhaps including you and I, could accept to dedicate some years of their lives as well as their finances to study at a university, hoping in that place to receive a new thought capable of helping them transform their society, once they arrived to it. With this kind of motivation, their excitement upon entering that university would certainly be understandable. But after acclimating themselves to the new environment and starting to feel they were part of it, they may have encountered a moment when they discovered a feeling of deception as they mingled with the senior students and professors. Perhaps they started to perceive they were actually not learning anything new, anything that wasn't already being used by the society, especially within the field they felt called to learn. And so instead of maintaining their excitement and inspiration through their years of study, they progressively became disillusioned, to the point where their zeal to transform the society became a desire to contribute to society and perhaps eventually to just provide for their own survival and well-being.

Indeed, if your own young soul did experience this profound shift of direction, it must have been disturbing to see this process occurring within yourself. But after passing through this mutation and re-evaluating your desires, you perhaps resolved to accept the situation as your fate, giving up your quest to understand the meaning of life, which you thought philosophy might explain. And in order to not lose all of your investment of time and money, you may have decided to just try to memorize the material, with a focus on earning high grades and passing your exams.

Surely, when we look at the original motivation of any person who tries to study philosophy and its related fields, we can recognize this motivation as beautiful and honorable. But perhaps because we felt we were not receiving what we were promised in order to fulfill our dream of transforming society, we lost the desire of our inner being, which was to help people. And, at the conclusion of our studies, many of us found ourselves questioning what we learned after reading the works of so many philosophers, and perhaps observed that our questions did not uncover the answers but mainly led to more questions.

Yet, because we did not want to appear unintelligent in the eyes of the ones who expected to see intelligence in us, like the professors at our university, we may have passed over our questions and instead tried to acquire learning without thinking too much about what everything meant. Surely we knew that to admit our incomprehension of what the philosophers were trying to say would not be well received by our professors, and due to that we might not be qualified to receive our degree. Therefore, for a multitude of reasons, it would not have been wise to say we did not understand, but rather, better to affirm that we did understand, in the name of pleasing our professors who believed in what they were teaching and our parents who wanted to see their children educated, and as well for ourselves who desperately wanted a degree for our future survival.

But regardless of our submission to this situation, perhaps our questions persisted in the unseen realms of our minds, namely the questions of how various philosophies could be applied to society as a whole, as well as what these philosophies had to do with anyone's personal life. Yet after all, because of the complexity of these philosophies, we perhaps found ourselves forgetting what we studied and just acting upon our original, instinctive concept of life. And reflecting on our long years of study, we may even have come to the conclusion that philosophy was difficult to understand because there was actually so little to understand.

After describing the painful reality of many students, shouldn't we also question what is happening in our institutions of learning that can cause students to experience such disillusionment? How is it possible that the students are not elevated and inspired by the words they study, the words that the pioneers of the ancient days promoted in order to create illumination? At this point, shouldn't we look more closely at the philosophies being studied?

It would certainly be nice if we could meet those philosophers of old, and have a chance to talk to them personally at their strong wooden tables. They would surely tell us the reason human beings in their day behaved barbarically was because they were unenlightened, and therefore they felt a duty to find a philosophy that could be used to change their society, hoping the thought they created would bring order and peace.

Then, with the awareness of what these philosophers wanted to achieve, should we not observe whether the students who learn their philosophies actually arrive to a state of having a more peaceful and hopeful behavior? If those students as individuals do become more peaceful, then we would have proof that the philosophies they learn have a good effect upon them and therefore could have a good effect on the society when those students try to proliferate what they had learned.

If, however, the effect on the students' behavior is negative, it would be normal to analyze more deeply the nature of the philosophies being taught in the forum of the university. As an analogy, if we eat a food that is not good, it is normal that our stomachs will have a reaction; similarly, if the students lose their positive desire, this means the philosophies they study must contain an inherently destructive element that could create this effect of demoralizing and destroying their enthusiasm, to the point that they do not just lose enthusiasm but develop as well a cynical mind. Indeed, the progressive discontentment that the students develop in their study halls could lead them to withdraw their involvement from the society that they initially wanted to elevate, or to want to dispute every issue at the political round-table, or even to become revolutionaries and take their fight to the streets, instead of becoming persons who are peaceful.

Interestingly, the parents of these students may be the first to remark upon the changes they see in their child, especially if they compare their child from the time he entered university to after he graduated. One thing they might notice is that their child no longer regards them with the same respect as they had educated him to have. Before entering university, their child was calm and gave recognition to them, and therefore they had many pleasant moments together that looked quite civilized. But after being educated in a variety of philosophical thoughts, this child who was growing into adulthood began step-by-step to act in a way where the parents could no longer perceive the reign of calmness in him or her, but instead perceived agitation and rebellion.

Indeed, if we look at what these young souls go through, we will realize that many students absorb the thought contained within the material they study, to a degree that it becomes part of their personality. It may accentuate certain characteristics in them to the point that their parents can recognize a drastic change in them, especially when they try to relate with them. And if by accident they make a remark to their child about his transformation, this student/child will first deny there is any change and will say that everything is fine with him and with the school he is attending. But if for some reason, the parents insist and describe some of his new behaviors, like being more agitated and less respectful, he will manifest his new behavior so aggressively that the parents will be afraid to come close to him again. This young person may interpret their remarks as an attack upon himself as well as upon his university, and as a result he might completely reject his parents as the price he has to pay in order to keep his conversion to a higher evolution. In any case, this student will no longer feel he has to agree with his parents, because he feels he is starting to see a new reality, something he did not know when he was with his parents or in his previous school.

One thing is for sure, when parents see their child begin to rebel and reject everything they have valued as good, I think the parents have difficulty to regard this kind of behavior as civilized or knowledgeable. They certainly will not consider this behavior could have been gained by accident. After experiencing this kind of situation, they might feel they were misled into giving their child away and financing an institution that was reputed to be a good university. Therefore, if many parents see this kind of result, surely we need to research the cause of this change in the attitude of the youths, especially when we know they were previously, to some degree, clear about life and clear in their desires. And beyond the elegance of the buildings, we should evaluate the training in that school, which demands the students to pass through a re-education process that makes them become critical about life and confused about who they are.

Origin of Philosophies

What is it about the philosophical realm that gives it such power to transform the character of a student? Indeed, when we research the origins of philosophy, we realize that behind each philosophy was a person who lived within certain circumstances and experienced feelings and thoughts connected to his time. In other words, every thought within a philosophy comes from a human being, not just as an inspiration from 'out of the blue'. We can say that a philosopher's thought actually came from what was close and dear to him, from his own body's behavior.

It would be interesting if some person who was known as a philosopher came to visit your table in your little local coffee shop and started to talk to you. Surely after listening to him, I absolutely believe you would not consider him to be a philosopher, but would just see him as someone who liked to chat and give his thoughts to you. And if you asked him where this thought he was expounding upon came from, he would reply that it came from his own mind, not from some far-away, outside inspiration.

So, we can say that a philosophy must come from the wellspring of someone's mind, and this well or this source is connected to someone physical on this earth. We can say that a philosophy must come from the body of someone, similar to spring water coming out from a rock. But what is maybe special about this 'philosopher' is that he has nurtured a talent for speaking and writing about his feelings and ideas. Based on this talent he has learned to manipulate words in such a mysterious and complex way that his presentation will be regarded by some as highly intelligent. Subsequently, in view of the quantity of ingredients composing his ideas, surely some university professors will be tempted to include his philosophy as additional material for their classes, and eventually to give it a place in the curriculum of their courses.

If we look at the process by which a philosopher creates his thoughts and comes to his conclusions, we will notice that when a philosopher examines different issues, the first thing he does is to find within himself an abundance of questions toward whatever he sees or hears. And if other people around are observing him, surely they will be fascinated, not just because his questions are interesting in themselves but because he generates so many more questions than other people do. Therefore these people will begin to compare the philosopher's mental aspect with their own and might make the conclusion that because they are not capable of generating so many questions, they must be 'simple people' or less educated people, while the philosopher with his mass of questions surely has an extra intelligence and must come from a higher class.

Due to this reputation of having surpassed the level of most people, the listeners may start to value and respect this philosopher as the most intelligent person they ever encountered, regardless he may have no answers to his mass of questions. Because he receives so much admiration and feels lifted by the people around him, this thinker will be stimulated to use his creative mind to work harder to find even more questions. And based on his ability to manipulate thoughts, this person will eventually develop, as an answer to some of his questions, a theory that looks like an ingenious thought.

However, as we examine his words in order to find the origin of his thought, we might realize that this philosopher actually did not understand many of the situations that surrounded him, but rather his expertise was in formulating questions about those situations. Surely he did have the ability to expose his questions and propose some answers, but if we analyze those answers to some degree, we will realize this philosopher gave only vague conclusions that were difficult to understand, especially for those who have the tendency to want to view the things around their lives with a positive approach. But for those who have a tendency to be negative or pessimistic, then surely this kind of thinker can stimulate their minds, because this thinker can find negativity in the smallest incident, similar to a person who struggles to get to work on time and blames the government for his difficulties, which on a scale of negativity seems to surpass the norm.

Philosophy of Marxism

Let us look at one of the most influential philosophers of the last century, whom I feel obliged to mention, namely Karl Marx. When we look at Marx's biography, it is clear that many events were taking place in his society as well as in his personal life that he did not understand or accept and which provoked him to question many things. But what is interesting is that the more he questioned the events surrounding his life, the more complex his theories became. And based on their complexity, his numerous articles and books were perceived as a great achievement by many people who had the same tendencies.

But if we try to comprehend Marx's writings with the intention of learning something that can be productive and hopeful in the direction of peace, we will not be able to find this nature in them. Marx's theory of the dialectic carried a sense of promoting conflict to create revolution, rather than a sense of promoting harmony to create evolution. And those who were attracted to study his voluminous writings did eventually develop a feeling that was quite opposite to the desire for peace.

So if philosophies of this kind are in the midst of our universities, then indeed the intense study of them will produce some damage on the part of the students. Indeed, if we are not aware of the influence that a thought can produce in our feelings, then we will choose to read words from anywhere, believing they are just words, without checking carefully the content. And because a student usually has the characteristic of being aggressive to study, he will not just read lightly but will amass the words inside his brain, to the point, without maybe realizing, his feelings will be affected.

Due to the ability of students to read many books and listen to many lectures in order to receive their degree, they do not usually perceive the depth of the connection between the words they read and the feelings they experience within themselves. But we can say that if a student, a researcher or even a casual reader becomes interested in a book that was written a hundred years ago or more, he should be aware that whatever feeling he has in the present moment can change according to what he reads and to the degree of his involvement with it, regardless that book was written at a different time of history.

We can question, how is it possible we can have a feeling about something that was written a hundred years earlier? Is it possible the feeling is trapped within the words of that author, like an insect is trapped inside the amber colored sap of a pine tree? If that is the case, then anyone who reads a book will not just find some descriptive words but will also release and revive the feelings captured within those words, regardless the author has been dead for a long time

Therefore if we give to students the writings of a philosopher like Karl Marx or some of his fellow philosophers, surely these students will be able to experience the actual feelings of these philosophers, to the point they will feel they can agree with these writers and disagree with everyone else.

Based on how much they agree with these philosophers, they may not be able to keep their former feelings, and that is why we will say they experienced a conversion. Indeed, these avid students can move through a process of absorbing Marx's thought to such a degree that they are able to actually receive the same emotions as Marx had at the time when he was writing those words, to a point where they are able to testify emotionally that his writings are true. But what is not said is that the emotional state they feel after studying his writings is not peace and happiness but obsession, confusion and even waves of depression, as perceived in the famous apostles of Karl Marx whom we call Stalin and Lenin, among many others.

Interestingly, most philosophers started their careers out of their concern for other people, who they perceived as being ignorant. In order to solve the dilemmas that they saw, they felt they could educate those people, and to do so they began to write and express their viewpoint. And the more they expressed their view of the situations around them, the more they found frustration about what they saw. Due to their augmenting frustration, their theories could drastically change from moderate to extremist.

Indeed, as the development of their philosophical imagination grew, little by little they started to value themselves as highly intelligent, regardless that their feelings of depression, delusion and low self-esteem were also increasing. To cover the invisible reality of their feelings, they were stimulated to expand their writings, to the point they eventually came to the stage where their thoughts made them feel so heavy and in such low esteem that a slow process of self-destruction was inevitable. At the same time, in order to lose awareness of what was happening to them, they often developed an intensity of behavior such as smoking, drinking or drugs. But regardless what levels of invisible emotion these writers were going through, on the intellectual side they continued to refine the quality of their words, wanting to believe that their thought was valuable and capable of influencing the world, as Karl Marx's philosophy in fact did, to the point where some people even considered him to be a key person in directing the course of history.

Yet even though these new philosophers brought what may have seemed like a revival, and regardless that their mass of questions fascinated people, we can conclude that they were incapable of finding suitable answers that could build something. Instead, the proposals contained within their writing were always that in order to promote an evolution of the world, we first have to remove what exists, and after that we can build something better.

Indeed, if we really study their writings, we can see that they were unable to respond positively to the problems of humanity, and many times, as individuals, they were blocked from dealing with their feelings toward what existed around their lives. To balance this deficiency, they continued to produce questions without any answers. Still bearing their frustrated desire to create a revolutionary thought, they must have come to a level where their feeling contained nothing positive and their last questions became, 'What is the purpose of my life?' and 'What is the purpose of other people's lives?'

Certainly in Marx's case, we can find through his writings that he must have found that zero point of no longer having positive feelings within himself. To discover how he came to this stage of feeling, we should observe carefully his theory of dialectical materialism, and we surely can perceive this theory did not arise from a heart that was full of joy. Instead it is understandable that his heart must have been in turmoil and empty to the point he was so thirsty he would want to destroy anyone who had water to drink, which explains why many people who adopted his philosophy also became thirsty to destroy themselves as well as anyone in the society around them.

The Egocentric 'I'

Now I would like to show you a way to look at philosophies from a slightly different angle. It is true that most philosophers had a certain way of seeing things, which other people in their time did not have. But if we closely observe what they were writing, we will realize that what they were presenting through their writings came from a part of their mind whose only desire was to promote its own self. And through the development of their ability to express themselves, they could begin to perceive a nature that I will call the egocentric 'I'.

Based on the pressure of this 'I', these individuals were eager and enthusiastic to share their discoveries with anyone around them who would listen. And what is interesting is that the more they expressed their 'I' to others and to themselves, the more this egocentric 'I' expressed the desire to reject anything that was not directly connected to satisfying its own self. As well, the more people began to follow that philosophy, the more those philosophers felt inspired to promote it as a great thought that could promote evolution. But when they encountered others who rejected their philosophy, feelings of frustration started to manifest within them to the point that they were ready to begin a revolution in order to eliminate the group of people who did not accept the new philosophy that they had 'discovered'.

Regardless what caused them to uphold this egocentric 'I', the belief that it was the right thought produced within them a lot of friction, which had the effect of deadening their senses to a level where they no longer felt the need for other people around them to exist. This explains why they could act with so much rejection and as well so much violence toward people. Since an egocentric character can quickly develop itself if a person adheres to an egocentric philosophy, this can explain why a person could arrive to the point where he has lost any sense that would permit him to value another person. Because of the loss of this sense, he could come to the point of considering it was right to kill other human beings in cold blood.

Indeed, if a human being makes it his vocation to develop the 'I', he will no longer be able to hear his own conscience, which usually along the way tries to warn him not to act upon the thoughts and feelings of the 'I'. And if this voice of conscience is not sufficient, surely some people would risk approaching him to suggest to him that the effect of the road of the 'I' would be to hurt him and others more than to promote something good, as he was thinking; but the chances are he would also reject these people.

What many philosophers and the people who were fascinated by them did not know was that in promoting the viewpoint of their egocentric mind, they were not only deadening their consciences, but they were putting themselves, knowingly or unknowingly, on the same level as the One who created everything in the universe, whom we usually call God. And because these philosophers put themselves equal to God or even above Him by promoting the primacy of their egocentric 'I', they blocked their eyes from seeing the wisdom of the harmoniousw processes of life that were taking place around them, and instead developed philosophies antagonistic to these natural processes.

As a result of the changes that occurred in them because of the promotion of the 'I', they began to develop a sense of being bothered by any philosophy supporting the existence of an Origin or bothered by any religion that looked like it upheld a belief in God. Based on the multitude of conflicting reactions within themselves, these philosophers came to stand in opposition to God, which surely made it impossible for them to understand the mind and the processes of God. Instead, because of their position of rivalry in relation to God, they were in the perfect place to question everything that exists in connection to God and to humanity, without fear.

If these philosophers who promoted the development of the egocentric 'I' could allow themselves to have a debate, face to face, with the students who chose to study what they wrote, one of the questions the students might ask to these philosophers would be if they believed in a heavenly God, or if they could hear that God, or just simply, if they could hear their conscience. After hearing these questions, these philosophers might proudly answer, "No, I don't believe in God," or they might declare, as if it were an honor, "I do not hear God speaking to me."

But they would not tell these students the reason they did not experience to hear the God of goodness speak, simply because they may not have known the reason themselves. What is shocking is that instead of feeling bad to have lost the dignity of being able to relate in some way with God, they would proudly respond that they did not believe in God. And in order to impress those students with their great superiority, they would tell them, "You know, it is clear that since God does not talk to me, He does not exist." And this was their great discovery.

Through their answers, it is obvious that the good God was not part of themselves. On the other hand, we can see they must have found another god, a god who can relate with the egocentric 'I'. Because of this, if a student dared to continue to question them by asking, "Do you understand people who believe in God?" these philosophers might become very emotional and rebuke them by answering, "I am not like those who believe in God; I am not a hypocrite like them, I am sincere."

Surely if philosophers of the theory of egocentricity worked hard to become one with the origin of this 'I', it does seem normal that they would believe they were the almighty 'I', or the only 'I'. And due to this position of absoluteness, they would not be able to hear the voice of the God of goodness. From this viewpoint, it is understandable as well that a person who follows a philosopher who promotes the right to be egocentric would also not be able to feel that good God. And if this person did feel something from time to time, for whatever reason, I think he would be forced to reject it because his philosophy would not allow anyone else to exist around him besides the 'I'.

After describing the effect of the philosophy of 'I', we can understand where Marx was standing, especially in connection to God's idea, which is always to promote life. Due to his discovery of the 'I', Marx's obsession became elevated to the level where he was against everything that could carry life, like God and like human beings who wished to meet God. Therefore the people who were following Marx's philosophy -- like Stalin, Lenin, and many other disciples -- had the objective of destroying both the flesh and the spirit of religious people, because they felt these people were against them.

If a philosopher was mainly writing with a heart of resentment toward God and anyone who promoted the idea of God, it is normal for the students who study the words of that philosopher to gradually develop feelings of being anti-God. And because of that these students will discover they feel more comfortable with people who are against God than with people who believe in God. Due to their standpoint, they will gain a cynicism that will cause them to become anti-life as well as anti-self, which will make them become anti-relationship toward people as well.

If people develop the egocentric 'I', this will block their senses toward what is around them and toward the invisible dimension of God, which will lead them into isolation. Because the 'I' demands people to first reject God and then to reject other people, eventually they will reject their own selves.

Students of the philosophy of 'I' will come to the point where they perceive everything around them as belonging to them, because they have concluded that God does not exist and nothing was created by God. And if the entire population of the world believes in the thought of the egocentric 'I', everyone will want to be the focal point. They will be busy all day long to satisfy their egocentric 'I', which will make this population endlessly hungry. If the entire world becomes this way, always hungry, what kind of nation and world will that be, a peaceful world or the opposite of peaceful?

Even if we do not fully know the meaning of what is good and bad, we can surely say the philosophy of 'I' is able to make people reach a state of depression that could become unbearable. In conclusion, we can say that a philosophy of 'I' has the ability to build an intellectual network of depression and create perfect revolutionaries, ready to inflame every land or every nation. And these revolutionaries are usually prepared to suffer in order to install their philosophy of 'I' in every land, and not averse to inflicting suffering on the people of that land.

Therefore, in order to give hope to the ones who are suffering due to this egocentric thought, the leader of that revolutionary group will promote a therapy to help them to not feel their own pain, which is to attack others who do not agree with them, and to attack them as violently as the pain they have inside themselves. Accordingly, immense masses of people can begin to accept to do violence to others, which they can do without remorse but with a sense of redemption.

Based on a dual motivation of promoting the 'I' philosophy plus finding the way to release themselves from the pain, these human beings are able to remove or to destroy the lives of others, which we know happened on a large scale in the so-named Red Revolution of Communism of 1917 and Mao's revolution in China, plus many other revolutions that have filled up this planet Earth's history through thousands of years.

To summarize, we can say, regardless Karl Marx did look like a genius from the viewpoint of knowing how to manipulate words, he also became the champion of secretly promoting the philosophy of 'I' as the new 'right', which demands as its first condition to remove any knowledge that would allow human beings to be aware that God can exist.

As a second condition of this egocentricity, he also promoted the sense of competition or conflict in order to create evolution, and he removed the value of those who were in leadership positions by promoting the need to vilify those persons for whatever they did, in the hope of destroying their morale.

From these premises, Marx's philosophy changed the rights of human beings from the freedom to express thoughts to a denial of permission to think. Eventually his philosophy was the main engine that detonated many other philosophies that contain the same origin of the 'I' as the center.

The Philosophy of 'We'

Since there are philosophies of 'I', can there also be philosophies with a different direction?

Or are we all condemned to follow the egocentric 'I' in order to fulfill the dream of the one who created this nature?

Surely if no one found another philosophy besides the 'I', then human beings are condemned to always destroy what they have built or to remove what bothers them until the time when someone else removes them, for having been the cause of bothering someone.

Lucky are we, when we dig inside our history books, that we can find some few men who seem to have wanted to promote a different philosophy.

For example, we can find one scientist/philosopher, Sir Isaac Newton, who discovered that the universe worked based on certain laws, including the law of gravity. We can ask, when he found the law of gravity, did this discovery come from his own imagination or did he observe something that already existed much before his personal existence? When we read his writings, we can see that he accredited the laws he discovered as having been made by Someone whom he called the Creator or the Supreme Inventor. Surely after his long research, Sir Newton must have felt he was called to show to humankind, through his discoveries, how intricate some parts of God's mind can be.

Another person, Dr. Albert Einstein, also contributed immensely to the field of science. We can ask whether Einstein considered that his theories came from himself or if he discovered the laws that Someone had used to create this world. Einstein once said that the more he discovered the laws of the universe, the more he felt humility and admiration for the Creator: "My religion consists of a humble admiration of the illimitable superior spirit who reveals himself in the slight details we are able to perceive with our frail and feeble mind." Through this statement, we can see that he must have found the quality of humility within himself in order to admit that what he found was the knowledge of Someone else, and what he accomplished was only to uncover that knowledge. Because he recognized the Creator in the midst of his research, then surely the Creator became inspired by Dr. Einstein, to the point that this Creator could have desired to help him discover the mechanisms upon which this universe was created.

If Dr. Einstein and Sir Newton had thought that whenever they discovered something they alone were the authors of their discoveries, they would have put the sole emphasis on themselves as the most eminent thinkers and therefore the most advanced human beings, to the point they would have upheld themselves as the 'I-myself' who created everything. Then every time these two men spoke, they would have begun their sentences with a big 'I', and surely it would have been impossible for God to continue to help them.

The reason God has difficulty to help the ones who use the 'I' is because this action makes them blind to the laws the Creator used in the creation. But because Newton and Einstein acknowledged there is a Creator to this universe, this humble approach permitted them to see what was previously unseen and it stimulated the desire and impetus within themselves to discover the universal laws that were operating around them.

Interestingly, we can realize that what these researchers discovered was not just the physical laws of the universe expressed through mathematics and physics, but in reality what they discovered was that nothing exists by itself and they were not alone. When these philosopher/scientists began to discern the mechanism of the building blocks of the universe and the forces that cause the interrelationships among atoms and molecules or between heavenly bodies, surely they must also have comprehended that a similar process enables human beings to progress, through two or more poles interacting and coming together in harmony.

By applying this view of distinct entities merging to become one, we can open a new way to perceive life, as well as to create our lives, which I call the Philosophy of 'We'. In this theory of 'We', we can observe that to form the 'We' identity, we need to have two or more individual identities that fuse into one. Based on the laws of science, we can consider that this theory of 'We' explains the processes of matter, and as well this theory can be viewed as the philosophy that tells us human beings that we need two poles to sustain ourselves and to progress to a higher and bigger identity, instead of thinking we exist alone as self-sufficient poles.

Due to this new combination of 'one self plus another self', or 'one self plus the One above', we can become people who have completely fulfilled our potential. From this standpoint, we can say these two researchers actually brought to humanity the philosophy that we need another pole so we as one pole can become one with that other pole in order to create a new identity. Based on this disclosure, which is demonstrated through the laws of physics, they allowed us to understand that within one identity there are actually two identities, like within one atom there are two kinds of charges, or within one molecule there are charged atoms.

By discovering the mechanisms of the physical world, these scientists helped humanity to elevate themselves to a higher capability and potential. Their discoveries allowed human beings to create new inventions and structures, and enabled us to be better able to fix our bodies, which are so many times damaged by sickness. Through this knowledge, we human beings have become better able to perceive the relationships between the physical, mental and emotional sides of ourselves, allowing us to more deeply respect and admire the identity of God through ourselves.

By comparison, if a scientist were to choose the philosophy of 'I' as the basic law of the universe and tried to create an atom in his laboratory based on this theory, it would be impossible because he would have to choose either an electron or a proton but not both. This is the reason no scientist can accept the philosophy of 'I' as a sustaining theory for our physical existence.

In the same manner, we can say the theory of 'I' cannot have arisen from the God of goodness who created the laws of the physical world of matter. From this perspective, it is logical to say that the theory of 'I' is not a true theory because it is impossible to create anything physically with it. More than that, this philosophy of 'I' must be a false theory whose only objective is to stop the process and the growth of our life's destiny, physically, mentally and emotionally. Regardless the theory of egocentrism is popular with the human character, this theory is an illusionary dream because it cannot create anything substantial, even though it may be presented as promoting something positive and better.

Based on knowing that the physical world has sustained itself for many millions of years through the philosophy of 'We', we can make the statement that the egocentric 'I' does have an objective, which is only to destroy people who believe in the philosophy of 'We'. The philosophy of 'I' wants to reject, isolate and denigrate any people who try to create a relationship with another being beside themselves. In general, we can say that the more we adhere to the philosophy of 'I', the more the 'I' will ask us to destroy any person who is trying to form an identity based on the 'We'.

The Rise and Fall of Civilizations

This fundamental struggle between the power of 'I' and the desire to follow the philosophy of 'We' can be observed in all the different civilizations. From a historian's point of view, it must be impressive and perplexing to see so many great cultures that arose and were so promising and ambitious in their time, only to decline after a few decades or centuries of progress and eventually be overtaken by the land they were previously standing on. Nevertheless, these civilizations left some remains to make us believe they did something impressive and important in their time. But after the historians and archaeologists have sifted through all these remains, they might finally come to the moment when they dig down to the question—What can be the reason for these great civilizations to have ended in this kind of manner?

We can suppose that if Sir Newton and Dr. Einstein had turned their energies to observing the history of civilizations, then with their analytical minds they could have found the laws that would permit civilizations to develop and to maintain their development. As well, they could have progressed to the logical conclusion that the civilizations that ended in ruin must have changed their philosophy in the course of their histories, in a way that served to promote destruction and the incapability to continue their growth, to the point where these civilizations returned to the sand.

But because these two scientists were focused on discovering the theories of how matter, energy and forces exist and interact, they were perhaps too busy to be able to perceive and apply the philosophical aspect of their theories to human civilizations.

If they had fully understood the applications of what they had discovered, they could also have deduced what kind of philosophy could destroy a civilization and cause it to fall, based on the laws of physics. Therefore these scientists would surely have been compelled to repel such a destructive philosophy for the simple reason that they knew it would promote the concept of 'opposition-promotes-evolution' as a power to advance the world, whereas their research had shown them that when two elements are in a harmonious relationship this will create a new level of matter, which means positive evolution. They knew that for the planet Earth with all of its life to be created, harmony between all of its poles had to be the core of its existence.

Indeed, if these scientists and many others could accept to create a philosophy for human existence with what they found in their scientific research, these individuals could have had the opportunity to confront the ones who initiated a philosophy of 'I' as redemption for the individual as well as for the society. Surely scientists would want to defend and promote life, and therefore they would have the power to stand before those persons who founded a destructive theory, because when we observe what science has discovered concerning the creation of all existence, we can say that even a proton carries within itself the philosophy of 'We'.

What is interesting about the philosophy of 'We' is that the word 'We' automatically includes us and someone else, and if we see ourselves as being part of one identity that is together with another identity, we will realize that we automatically choose the word 'we' when we refer to ourselves. The same is true for the word 'couple', which automatically refers to two individual identities within the couple. If we are part of a couple, we know when we say 'we' it represents us plus our partner. And if we choose to be part of another identity, for example a nation, then when we say 'we' it means we as individuals are representing the nation.

If we start to use this vocabulary of 'We' as part of our view of life, our daily emotional life will be transformed. Likewise, if a philosopher is using the concept of 'We' in his philosophy, then the feeling we receive when we read his view is drastically different from the feeling we receive from a writer who uses the theory of 'I'. Just using the word 'We' allows us to see everything with a large mind, and due to this view, we receive a positive feeling, which will make us want to be part of our civilization and part of our world.

If the archeologists and historians were to accept to recognize that there have been philosophies of 'I' as well as philosophies of 'We' which human beings could choose from, they would surely understand the reason a civilization could rise due to using a philosophy of 'We', as well as why it could decline. While digging through the artifacts of an ancient civilization, they could ascertain that for this certain civilization to rise and then decline, there must have been a dramatic switch in the theory that it adopted in the process of its history.

If a civilization like Greece, which appeared so prominent and well protected in social ways, could decline and fall, then surely our historians should question whether there was a force within that had the power to destabilize that civilization, even without any external war. Surely they could deduct that the only way to destroy that civilization was to introduce to its people a different philosophy from its founding philosophy, without those people understanding the danger of it.

Indeed, if in the midst of this civilization there was suddenly some person who brought the philosophy of 'I', surely this person would have presented it sweetly and smoothly, because the specialty of the philosophy of 'I' is to not demand any responsibility from the individual. Based on the sweet presentation of this philosophy of 'I', surely the people who had learned to sacrifice their lives for a greater goal must have suddenly felt that this philosophy extended their rights, to the point they could demand everything from others without having to do anything for others in return.

As we know, we too in our time come very close to being tempted, if not contaminated, by that philosophy of 'I' which demands others to live for us and us to live for nobody. And based on this philosophy, many symptoms of our society demonstrate a sickness that appears impossible to fix, especially when we promote the right to elevate the 'I' as more important than the whole. If this sickness becomes more wide-spread, then we know our civilization or maybe our world can return to the dark ages from whence it came. If that situation were to occur, many would interrogate their God, "Why has this happened to us, why do we look so sick, why can't we trust anybody?"

But I do believe their God would not have a problem to respond to them, not by giving an answer, but by asking the question of them, "What philosophy did you choose that could make you so sick?"

From these observations, any civilization that does not revolve around the theory of 'We' has little chance to survive and continually prosper, as it wishes. In other words, when people in a specific civilization do not choose a philosophy or theory that recognizes others besides themselves, this civilization will only pursue individual happiness without consideration of the happiness of others, which will inevitably lead it into despair.

In recent history there have been certain countries where the status of living became tremendously deficient. If we analyze the reason for this deficiency, based on the philosophies we have examined so far, we can understand that within these regions or countries there must have been a theory that made every living thing incapable of progressing. In this case we can say the philosophy of these countries was based on a theory that would inevitably produce deficiencies and shortages, in other words, based on a philosophy of 'I', which contains the strength to remove the energy necessary for life or progression.

Regardless the symptoms of the philosophy of 'I' do not look good, the reason many people choose the philosophy of 'I' is because they believe it can allow them to protect themselves more than if they use the philosophy of 'We'. Often people have a tendency to anticipate that nobody will take care of them, leading them to take all kinds of measures to ensure their survival.

So regardless it was a philosophy of 'We' that allowed a country to rise, after awhile the people may accept some doctor of 'I' to promote his philosophy in their midst, to the point the indoctrination from this doctor becomes a temptation. Due to this infiltration the people begin to want to be taken care of, and eventually they can conclude that the best way is to take care of themselves by themselves. They believe that the philosophy of 'We' will make them poor and vulnerable, because they know it teaches that individuals need to take care of others before they take care of themselves. In the midst of a country that earlier knew the only way to survive was to take care of each other, the minds of the people influenced by a philosophy of 'I' will become weaker and weaker, to the point the people feel indeed the only way to survive is to take care of themselves. Surely, if the doctors of the philosophy of 'I' have done their work well, people will eventually feel that the philosophy of 'We' looks unattractive and unrealistic.

Indeed, by accepting the theory of 'I' and rejecting the theory of 'We', the individuals in a nation will dive down into the depths of the philosophy of 'I', until the fall of the people becomes evident as the fall of the country. Due to the change in their viewpoint, the people will have less comprehension of the capacity of the 'We', and their degree of strength will also lessen, because they will arrive to a realm that looks like the bottom of the ocean where only a little amount of light can arrive. When this nation descends to such a level, surely they will not be able to rise until they have removed the philosophy that sent them to the bottom of the ocean.

Necessity of the Philosophy of 'We'

The fact is, when we observe civilizations or nations in the early stages of their development, we can see that the people must have chosen the philosophy of 'We', and this ideal allowed them to survive the difficult early stages. Through being educated with the thought of 'We', the people could choose to be part of a larger group, perhaps with a motto of, 'We the people of this nation can form one family where differences like color, race or gender will not be an issue,' and therefore they could emerge as a new civilization. Surely at this point, people must have felt honor and enthusiasm to the point they wanted to say 'thanks' to their God for having blessed them.

But after years passed, perhaps the citizens of this country did not value their philosophy as much and forgot the original intentions of their forefathers. Because of that they began to tilt to a new philosophy that asked, "Why are you working so hard? Your country is rich; why don't you take from your country what you should have gained?"

In the moment people start to take the philosophy of wanting to be served or rewarded, the nation will shift to a downward slope. In this process, the people will remove the belief that they should give themselves for the sake of others and they will begin instead to believe that others should take care of them. Instead of viewing that others are necessary for their survival, they will begin to see others as an obstacle to their survival. Surely as this attitude begins to appear, it will lead them on a new road that inevitably will send their civilization to the bottom of the ocean, as in the story of Atlantis.

Based on this symbolic city that disappeared, the people can know the depths of where the philosophy of 'I' can lead them, and perhaps they can perceive their life disappearing as if it were going down a hole, similar to a place in the universe we call a black hole. And when the people who are falling arrive at the edge of that hole, they might be able to know where they are when they hear some words warning them: "This is as far as you should go because if you don't stop here, you will surely destroy yourselves."

Unfortunately, as the philosophy of 'I' starts to increase its demands inside of the people of a nation, they usually do not see the danger ahead. They do not perceive that the philosophy of 'I' is causing them to have feelings of anxiety that provoke pain, and they create pain relievers and sleeping pills to try to remove their symptoms. But regardless they take their prescriptions, the pain will continue to grow within themselves and others to the point where the desire to destroy themselves becomes acceptable or inevitable, and their civilization's decline is assured.

In connection to our personal reality, the philosophy of 'I' has the power to impoverish us too, just by removing the 'We'. The egocentric 'I' has the power to dismantle our ability to produce thoughts that create joy, and block us from being sensitive to the energy necessary for our development. And when human beings have no energy to exchange with one another, there can be no love for each other and no wish to live for each other. Instead, because we become so drained in the end, our emotional demands will force us to drain energy from someone who has energy, if there is someone left.

However, if you have the chance to meet a person who has pursued the theory of 'We' in his or her life, you will discover this person looks peaceful, happy and joyful, and has a lot of creativity. He will have a well-nourished character, and surely will not feel fear or aggression whenever he meets someone. Instead, this person will be able to welcome any person who comes close to him, and this meeting will be seen as fruitful or productive or simply a peaceful time they both can enjoy together. The people who meet a person who follows the philosophy of 'We' usually desire to stay close to him or her. They do not want to leave this person's presence after one minute or even one hour. In fact, the person who lives according to the philosophy of 'We' makes us feel so good that we may want to stay with him or her for an endless period of time.

Surely we can say every human being wishes to experience this feeling of wanting to stay with someone forever. This is the reason people have a tendency to pledge to each other their desire to live for the other one for eternity or 'until death do us part'. In contrast, if you approach a person who carries the philosophy of 'I' as his center, you will perceive he is extremely narrow-minded and will be difficult to live with, and you will not want to make this kind of pledge.

How to Promote the 'We' in our Lives

So how can we use the philosophy of 'We' to become a person that others will want to stay with? What do we need to do to create that character in ourselves?

Well, let's start with a familiar scene, like when you are visiting a nearby park. If you walk around this park and look at everything with the viewpoint of the philosophy of 'I', you might be saying to yourself, "Oh, nice flowers" or "Hmm, big trees," and after walking along the paths with this philosophy in your mind for ten minutes or more, you will find the feeling of boredom starting to emerge.

On the other hand, if you go to a park with the idea of choosing the philosophy of 'We', it means you accept to include someone with you, even if no other person is physically present at that moment. You can eventually find a partner like God to be with you and you can look at the park together with Him. As you recognize the presence of duality by thinking, "We see the trees" or "We are looking at the flowers", your feelings will increase.

From the moment you include the presence of another beside yourself as part of your 'We', you will be amazed by the feelings that come to you.

So, if you decide to be one of those persons who aspire to follow the demands of the philosophy of 'We', you will need to choose someone in addition to yourself as the other pole. And what is interesting is that what you choose as the other pole will affect your degree of feeling. For example, you can say, 'I plus my dog', and get a certain amount of feeling, or 'I plus my students' and get more, or 'I plus my partner' and receive a deeper feeling. If you desire to amplify your feeling to the highest degree, you might consider saying, 'I plus Jesus' or 'I plus God' as the 'We'. Who you choose as the one to make duality with will define the quantity and quality of the emotion you receive.

What causes these different feelings? When a person looks at the flowers in the park with an egocentric viewpoint, he will not acknowledge the Creator of the flowers, or the landscape designer or the gardener who takes care of them, to the point this person will feel the garden is not extraordinary. But if this same person chooses the theory of 'We' as his viewpoint, he will acknowledge the Creator of everything, and this view will allow him to see how many things are created in pairs or from two individual poles, in order to create beauty. And when he observes the created world around him, he will not only appreciate the objects but he will easily accept to say, 'Thank you' to God.

But a person who is printed with the philosophy of 'I' will automatically remove anyone or anything that represents another pole, without even consciously knowing he is doing that. As a result, this person will feel it is normal to not acknowledge a Creator or any other person who has participated in the well-being of his life. He will not feel strange to remove them from his consciousness. This person will question the importance of acknowledging God and eventually will ask, "What difference does it make if we do or do not acknowledge a Creator of all things?" He will also propose, "Don't you think our purpose on Earth is to consummate what the Earth has given to us for our personal use, instead of using our time to say 'thank you' to a Creator or to whoever participated in the creation of what we have?"

From the viewpoint of just acquiring the physical necessities of life, it is correct, the need to acknowledge the Creator or any person who contributes to our life is not necessary. But from the viewpoint of the world of emotion and to create a character of goodness, it will make a majestic difference if we recognize the One who created something before we consider that we can obtain it for our use. Regardless it may look like the demand of recognizing God and others is a gigantic effort, we can say that if we are interested in receiving feelings that can give us pleasure, the effort to always recognize another partner is much more rewarding in the long term than it is to reject our counterpart.

What we identify as a pleasurable feeling actually comes from the energy we receive by choosing the theory of 'two poles'. In contrast, when we choose the theory of 'one pole' or an egocentric thought, we are removing our capacity to receive positive energy and therefore are putting ourselves in a position where we will feel a lack of energy. This emotional situation is inevitable since the 'I' allows the right for only one pole to exist, and thereby forces anyone who carries this philosophy to be isolated, producing loneliness, emptiness, and eventually depression.

Therefore, if today human beings seem to have difficulty finding the place of perfect happiness, it may not be because the park where they are walking is lacking in beauty or because their car is not the latest model. It is because the philosophy of 'I' makes everything look ugly to people's eyes because it stops them from receiving love and filling up their souls. This situation is similar to a drinking glass with nothing in it or a plate that is empty. Regardless how beautiful these objects can be, they don't fulfill their real value until we fill up the cup and put some appetizing food on the plate.

What is interesting to observe is that even though our living and working environment today is improved immensely in comparison to previous centuries, we still hear human beings complaining about their surroundings, which shows us they must continue to carry the philosophy of 'I'. It is sad to see that even though we ameliorate our environment in many luxurious ways, nothing will please us human beings until we change our philosophy. And nothing a nation does can please its people until these people find the philosophy that satisfies their original heart.

You can be sure that if you train your mind to use the philosophy of 'We', you will be qualified to live harmoniously with all things that exist around you. And with the consciousness of you as an individual together with God forming the 'We' within yourself, you will also understand the need to find a physical partner with whom to create the building blocks of joy. Together with that partner, who of course also accepts to live according to the same philosophy of 'We', you will find the perfect environment to mature the love that insists on blossoming.

However, if instead of the 'We' you install the philosophy of 'I' in your head, you are forced to remove the other identity that would have permitted you to receive the energy necessary to create a relationship. If you use the theory of 'I' when you look at your partner, you are actually rejecting him or her in your mind. As a result that person will no longer exist for you, and due to that you will lose in a blink of an eye any feeling for her or him. At the same time, by not recognizing the other pole beside you, you inevitably will perceive feelings of emptiness manifesting themselves inside of you, making you feel alone and depressed.

To understand the power the 'I' has within us, we can say that when someone carries the philosophy of 'I,' his mind automatically questions what another pole is doing, for example, why a person does this or that. It is the power of the 'I' that demands to be the only one and rejects the other, who is seen as an extra identity besides himself. This person who carries the 'I' will question why this other pole exists or what it is doing there, because the 'I' only allows one pole the right to exist.

A person who chooses the philosophy of 'I' for whatever reason will start to experience confusion and turmoil, which will be portrayed as well through many physical behaviors. As a result it will be difficult for this person to identify himself as having a stable character. Due to the changeable feelings that are passing through his mind and body, he will always be concerned with fixing his feelings, as his first priority. This is the reason many human beings are looking everywhere for ways to repair themselves.

But one thing we have to remember: feelings of whatever category are only the effects of our thoughts. If a person is not examining the thoughts he uses in his daily life, he will always be incapable of solving his emotional situation, regardless of his wish. However, if he is able to recognize the thoughts he chooses as the cause of his emotional turmoil, that awareness can help him to minimize the belief that it is his destiny to always be subjected to those ups and downs of feeling as part of his character. And if this person chooses the philosophy of 'We' as his 'daily bread', he can go straight toward the fulfillment of his original heart.

Using the philosophy of 'We' will affect your life, step-by-step, even though your life might not change so much from the external aspect. But from the aspect of emotional development, you will be able to feel you are maturing, to a level where other persons will begin to notice and appreciate you. Surely if this event happens to you, you will be obliged to believe you did make a drastic change in comparison to what you used to be.

If you look carefully at the effect of your choice between the philosophy of 'I' and the philosophy of 'We', you will realize how easy it is to either build or to destroy the energy that is necessary to sustain life. When you choose to include another pole besides yourself, which means accepting a new situation or welcoming another person, you actually construct the base within yourself to permit the universal energy to come inside you in order to mature your internal being, which can be called your character of goodness. This energy will pass through your physical senses, and therefore it is normal that you can experience many feelings of pleasure with others.

From this viewpoint, we can see how much human beings are responsible for the choices they make and especially for the category of thoughts they have. They can choose to use the philosophy of 'We', which creates happiness and makes them more aware of God as well as the persons around them, or they can choose the philosophy of 'I', which makes them blind to any person they meet and surely makes them reject the existence of God.

Regardless we can believe that God has power over all things, we have to also accept to see that nothing happens by coincidence and that our destiny is our human responsibility, regardless it looks like we are vulnerable and easily influenced. The bottom line is, if you adopt the philosophy of 'I', nobody will take responsibility for your destiny, but instead people will say you hurt yourself. And surely when you approach the end of your life, you will realize deeply that you have been duped and there is nothing you can do except shift your direction as quickly as possible before you come to a stage where remorse will be your eternal feeling.

The Fulfillment of the Philosophy of 'We'

If we consider that life is just a moment we live on Earth and there is nothing coming after our time here, it is possible it doesn't matter what we do or what we choose as a philosophy for our life. But if we consider our life continues to exist after we shed our body, then we will feel remorse and sorrow for what we did to ourselves if we passed through our life without receiving the energy needed to mature our souls, and especially if we realize the life over there demands great energy. Therefore, instead of waiting to know what will happen after our physical life, it is wise to do the right thing for our soul during our physical life.

If there were someone who did profoundly address this issue of how to prepare ourselves during our physical life for the continuation of our life eternally, wouldn't it be wonderful? Certainly we would like to find a person who was absolutely committed to the philosophy of 'We' and who became the fulfillment of that philosophy. I surely will not hesitate to say, yes, there is someone who did promote this philosophy of 'We', and gained the highest doctoral degree in that subject. So I would like to introduce this person, whom I will call Dr. Jesus, with an apology to not know his family name.

When we read Dr. Jesus' words, we can find many expressions that show how deeply he recognized the two poles as his priority, with one pole representing himself and the other his Origin. Based on this awareness, we can comprehend why he said, "I am in the Father and the Father is in me" (John 14:10), and "Anyone who has seen me has seen the Father" (John 14:9). Through these statements, Dr. Jesus wanted to present what he considered to be the most honorable thought, which is to recognize the Father. And when we look at his life, we can see that because of this recognition of his Origin, he could stand firmly and without fear in front of other people, even in front of the high representatives of his religion and his nation. Because he saw himself together with the Father, his feelings were absolutely unshakeable and that is why he could endure all the negative events around his life.

As the record tells us, Dr. Jesus drew the attention of many people in his time, not only of his personal students, who could be called his disciples, but he also drew the attention of religious scholars, leaders and even kings. In order for a king who rules over many people to be impressed enough to want to meet Dr. Jesus, we can realize that Dr. Jesus must have built his life with a philosophy that created within him a deeply magnetic personality. Surely if he had used a different philosophy, like the philosophy of the 'I', he might have said, "When you see me, you see only me", or "I am because I think". If Dr. Jesus had actually presented himself this way to the people, I wonder if his students would have been inspired to listen to him or if they would have been repelled and ready to leave after a few minutes or hours.

When we examine the philosophy of Dr. Jesus, we realize how profoundly he promoted the philosophy of 'We' through his example of serving others and ultimately by dying for them, in order for the process of growth and salvation to be fulfilled. We can also perceive that he often asked the people living in his time to invite him into their midst, in order that they could receive the love they needed to love others. Dr. Jesus knew that everything around our lives functions based on the philosophy of 'We', and due to this theology he could make statements like, "Do to others as you would have them to do to you" (Matt 7:12) and "Whatever you do for one of the least of these brothers of mine, you do for me" (Matt 25:40). He even said that by inviting his presence with us, we would be able to perform miracles, which we can perceive as meaning that Dr. Jesus knew that transformation can come about only by living in duality with him.

But what is interesting is that, due to his thought that promoted the need to live for others, Dr. Jesus came to be perceived as the main public enemy in his time. For some reason, his words created fear and panic. This was primarily because people could sense that his philosophy was shaking and weakening the philosophy of 'I', or the egocentricity, that was inside of them and that they had built for so many years. However, instead of letting go of their old identity, which was based upon egocentricity, and allowing Dr. Jesus to achieve his task, they sought to retain their identity by re-fortifying their belief, which permitted them to justify themselves. And perhaps because they felt they were losing the argument, they began to seek a way to remove him in haste.

Indeed, through the events recorded in the book we call the Bible, we can perceive that the people who were around Dr. Jesus could not adopt his philosophy of 'We'. If they had accepted and adopted it, the first thing that would have happened is they would have stayed with him, especially when everything became difficult for him, and due to this protection the tragedy of Dr. Jesus' life would not have turned so bitter.

If Dr. Jesus' philosophy or message could not be welcomed, this means people around him must already have been deeply indoctrinated by another thought that was taking them down a road opposite to the 'We'. Contrary to Dr. Jesus' philosophy, there must have been many teachers at that time who promoted a theory of individual destiny or self-interest without valuing others as part of their salvation and growth or valuing an awareness of God's presence. And if the people were well educated by their teachers, surely the philosophy of personal survival was strong enough to blind them and block them from understanding and accepting the philosophy of Dr. Jesus.

If indeed the people of Dr. Jesus' time had been able to accept his words and accept him as an incarnation of those words, the society where he was living would surely have changed, to the point the Romans, who were interested in creating a lasting social order on earth, might have been happy to find a great thinker to keep their civilization progressing. But since Jesus' own people who had been educated by God directly through the prophets could not receive him and his words, the Romans as well were left with no philosophy that could give happiness to their citizens. They were obliged to keep listening to the voice that demanded them to value the philosophy of 'I' and which drove them eventually, as we know, to self-destruction some years after Dr. Jesus left from this side.

Due to the many difficulties that perpetually surrounded Dr. Jesus in his time, it must have been with much sorrow that he did not have time to write his doctorate. But regardless of what feelings he could have had, I consider that he is the true founder of the philosophy of 'We', and based on this qualification, I surely believe that if he could have had the right to express himself, he would have elaborated on this philosophy with all the power of persuasion and the elevated viewpoint that he possessed. Regrettably, many thoughts he intended to present to us, and even many that he was able to verbalize, could not be written down or were not written precisely enough to allow us to experience his presence fully. Because those ideas were not easy to comprehend, especially for those who did not have the same origin as Dr. Jesus, the disciples could not write them down exactly or the words were blended with the words of the disciples or of other writers, making it almost impossible to distinguish what Dr. Jesus really said from what the writer was able to understand or accept.

Therefore what we have today as a record is the thought of many different writers who did not fully understand Dr. Jesus or could not believe in him when he most needed them to believe in him. This is to say, those people who were the so-called first believers must still have been under the influence of the egocentric 'I', therefore whatever words they heard from Dr. Jesus were often manipulated. Another reason the disciples could have transformed what Dr. Jesus said was so those words could be understood by people who carried a different origin from Dr. Jesus himself. As a result, many of the thoughts written in the books of the New Testament promote one's own personal salvation, urging one to first consider oneself, which looks similar to what the philosophy of 'I' presents.

If you are one of those who today carry the philosophy of 'I' or the theory of being the only one who walks on this planet without seeing others, you may surely understand the feelings of the people of the time, especially after Dr. Jesus said, "Anyone who has seen me has seen the Father" (John 14:9). Surely if you hear this statement, which illustrates the extreme philosophy of 'We' in its absoluteness, you will feel anger as the people around Dr. Jesus must have felt. And if you recognize your reaction against these words, you can also understand the disciples' feelings when they were before Dr. Jesus. Due to these feelings, we can understand the reason Dr. Jesus found it difficult to be welcomed, because everywhere he spoke he was confronting the thought of egocentricity, which is connected with anger.

Origin of the Philosophy of 'I'

What can be the reason that people can have such rejection against this philosophy of 'We' or the theory of 'One-plus-One' from such a long time ago until today? How is it possible that human beings of today still have the potential to value the philosophy of 'I' as being so attractive, regardless we look so developed externally? Surely we can presume this attraction must come from some place deep within ourselves, a place where every human being is connected to something or someone egocentric as our origin.

If we look within our mind, however, we might not find the place where that philosophy of 'I' is rooted, because in our mind we can also find a persistent desire to live with others. Based on this, we can consider that if the egocentric philosophy of 'I' is not residing in our mind, we need to look deeper within our physical selves to find where this 'I' exists. Based on the research of our modern age, we know there is a place where everything is printed like a code, which we name DNA. Therefore, if the 'I' is rooted there, we can as well think we are in some way condemned to function according to its guidelines.

To see if we have DNA that is printed with the theory of 'I', or the thought of being the only one who counts, the best way to test this theory is to perform an experiment. If someone is asked to consider the philosophy of 'We' and responds positively right away, we can say the existence of the gene of 'I' is weak within that person. But if a person responds violently toward that philosophy or toward anything that demands him to make duality with someone or to help someone, then we can deduce he still carries a strong gene in his DNA that demands him to take the 'I' road.

Based on the discovery that the philosophy of 'I' could be printed in our DNA, we should not be surprised to find the continuation of egocentricity from old times up to today. Since egocentricity has the tendency to be stored in the human DNA, it is understandable why individual persons living at the time of Dr. Jesus could have enormous difficulty to accept certain words and events from his life. And as well, based on knowing that we could inherit this 'I' from birth, it is also understandable why we who are living so many years later would still have enormous difficulty to accept certain events from Dr. Jesus' life, such as his statements that he was one with the Father or that we have to include him in our life in order to follow the philosophy of 'We'.

Overall we can say, until the genes that continue to carry the 'I' are removed, it will be difficult for us to truly recognize Dr. Jesus or to believe in what he says. But regardless we have the gene that carries the 'I' as a dominant power, if we progressively make effort to believe in the philosophy of 'We' and act based upon it, we can print a new code in ourselves, which will help us to uproot the 'I' that is in our genes and replace it with the 'We'. And if this can take place within ourselves, surely we will be able to recognize Dr. Jesus as being in us, as he recognized his Father in him.

If we attentively take the philosophy of Dr. Jesus as the center of our life, we will realize the main reason he emphasized that we should value others and accept what is living around us was to help us create a new origin within our genes. This effort will not just replace the dominance of the 'I', it will also permit us to receive God's love freely. Until now, this love was living somewhere outside of ourselves but could not be perceived or received by us due to the fact that our genes printed with the 'I' always rejected the other pole that can form the 'We'. If we decide to live according to the law of duality that promotes the 'We', we will be able to receive God's love, which is waiting to be a part of us.

As well, if the people of the time of Dr. Jesus had been accepting of his philosophy of 'We' from the first, this would have helped them to accept his person, and this would have allowed them to be in the position where they could have directly received the love of God, which gradually would have made them into loveable beings as Dr. Jesus must have been. Surely if his direct students had welcomed him completely, they would have been able to recognize his love even more deeply, to the point they would not only have been in admiration of him, but they would have been able to experience the love that Dr. Jesus experienced.

So if today I bring back this philosophy of 'We' or this theory of 'Two', it is because what Dr. Jesus taught was absolutely revolutionary from the view of helping humankind to gain lives full of happiness inside our beings, in order to become beautiful gifts for others. In this respect, I do believe that any human being who accepts to introduce Dr. Jesus' philosophy into his mind will be able to experience the emotional effect many times over, allowing him or her to become more beautiful day by day. If someone makes daily effort on the road of living for another pole, he or she will become a person who is surely more welcomed than someone who always introduces him or herself as the almighty 'I' first. And surely we can have confidence to say, the person who makes effort to live according to the law of 'We' will have the quality to become a citizen of a kingdom where the heart reigns, instead of a citizen of a kingdom of misery, where the philosophy of 'I' imprisons us.

The truth is that if we look at what philosophies humans are following today, we surely can conclude that if Dr. Jesus could be here with us, he would still feel great concern for us. He would surely be happy if we would begin to follow his words and fulfill our internal desire, which after all is to receive love in order to become mature beings. And surely if this time we could welcome his progressive philosophy, he would be extremely pleased to know that we, the earthly people, had adopted the philosophy of 'We' for our lives, regardless he brought this theory over 2,000 years ago.

So, I hope, after having learned the characteristics of the philosophy of 'We', when you decide to go to the park, you will not look at everything as your property that belongs to you alone or to think that you are in the park and nothing exists besides you, but instead you will recognize the Pole necessary to receive the energy of heaven, which will allow you to fully admire the beautiful trees, etc. And if you are walking through the park together with your friend and acknowledge God to give you this friend, you will feel very happy to be with him or her, because God will be able to give you His love for your friend.

As well, if you look at your family with the philosophy of 'We', you will say 'thanks' to God for your family and therefore the love of God for them will always flow through you. And if the philosophy of 'We' could be taught in the universities, the faculty and students would be filled with the positive energy of God, and based on this energy the functioning of their minds would surely improve, helping them discover the intricacies of the creation, as well as laws of economy, politics and human interactions. If God could find an opening within the world of education, the university itself would be the best place for God's energy to dwell and therefore the best place to find inspiration, which the students originally came to the university to receive. And when those students graduate and go forth into the society, they would be a plus rather than a negative.

When we recognize both the Owner of the universe, which is God, and ourselves as His representatives on this Earth, then whatever exists around us will be taken care of, like a gardener takes care of his flower beds, and we will also qualify ourselves to be the owners of this wonderful planet, as well. If we want to have a world that is serene, joyful and lovely, it is an absolute necessity to re-enthrone God to the place where He should be and to recognize others as having the same value as ourselves. And I think if there is someone who can achieve this, God will be very much in love with this person. Finally, if all people agree with this philosophy, God will not limit Himself to love a few, but will come to give His love to all of humanity as well.

Based on this awareness, if a person accepts to live according to the philosophy of 'We' during his time on Earth, surely due to the mass of love he can receive, we can be confident that he will live where Dr. Jesus wants to see all humanity live. And if a family can use this philosophy, the children will say to the parents, "When I see my parents, I see God," the father will say, "When I see my wife, I see God," and his wife will say, "When I see my husband, I see God."

If everyone makes the effort to achieve that philosophy of 'We', every aspect of life will be filled with the love of Heaven, which will be circulating around the Earth like a cloud full of light, ready to envelop every home in order to create a society where love can dwell, like the sun brings the sunshine to our skin, or like the wind comes to help us to keep our flesh at the perfect temperature.

If all of us choose that road of 'We', surely we can say our society will rise, as well as our society will maintain for eternity. And surely Dr. Jesus will say, "This is the Kingdom of Heaven I wanted to see."

Symbols of God's Love

I believe people must notice their surroundings while they are walking around their downtown or through their local park, or while strolling in the countryside or hiking up a mountain, or as well, while visiting a tourist destination during their vacation. And as they observe the objects in their environment, they may start to develop ideas about how some of these things could be used.

For example, when they pass a bakery on a village street, thoughts may begin to form in their head such as, "Perhaps I should buy something from that bakery," or "I could bake something like that at my home," or even more adventurous, "Maybe I could create a little bakery just like this in my own hometown."

Indeed, many of the ideas and thoughts we form are based on physical things we have seen. Regardless our thoughts may begin because we see something, these thoughts can continue to develop into dreams, goals, or ambitions if we add some of our own desires and wishes. When the ingredients of these dreams and ambitions remain in our minds for some period of time, they can turn into beliefs, and eventually these beliefs can come to the point of amassing enough conviction to propel our bodies into action. If we make enough physical effort, our dreams can be accomplished, turning into the fulfillment of our goals. Through this process, we can create a new destiny for our physical lives.

In the example of passing the bakery, maybe the person, if it was you, had the thought of buying something from that little bakery. Maybe you thought that you would like to find a recipe to make something similar to a fruit-filled pastry you saw on the shelves of that bakery, or even imagined that you would find the way to create a little bakery of your own in your neighborhood. In each of these cases, you can consider the idea coming to you as a goal, but regardless your idea can be transformed into a goal, to achieve it you must decide to do something physically. From this viewpoint, if anyone accepts to make a goal, this person will need to not escape from the various difficulties that arise in the process of achieving that goal.

Let us look at another kind of example, like a medical researcher who believes he can find a solution to a particular illness. Although he has the dream of discovering a cure, many dilemmas will arise between the time of formulating his idea, until the time when he actually discovers the cure in a substantial and material way.

First, the researcher must begin to work toward understanding how the illness originates and functions, with the hope that by knowing its mechanics he can obtain some clues to discover the knowledge he needs to help him create the cure. At the same time he must maintain the belief in his head that he can find the cure for this particular illness. If he loses this belief, he will automatically be unable to continue. Although a person such as this has a strong ambition and goal to help other human beings, he must first gain specific qualifications of knowledge and, above all, he has to gain a certain stability within his character in order to pass through the multitude of difficulties that he is sure to encounter along the way without being discouraged.

We can say that the first qualification a researcher of any kind must have is the ability to maintain faith in his ultimate goal, because during the long process of research he will experience a multitude of doubts coming to him, especially if he meets a wall while performing some experiments. Often the most difficult time to keep faith is when the cure is close to being discovered. His faith can be shattered at that moment because he has already endured a great length of time to come to the point where he is, and because he feels he is near the end, he suddenly wants everything he is doing to go fast, and due to the acceleration of his wish, he begins to struggle with his faith.

From this situation we can remark that in order to achieve something physical, no matter what, there is a high demand for a specific character, composed of both a quality of thought and a certain amount of faith in order to successfully fulfill the time period that is necessary to find the desired result.

In addition to the tenacity needed to maintain faith, a second qualification is also required from the researcher, which is the persistence to physically work hard. If a researcher has these two qualities, he will eventually be able to narrow the gap between where he began, which was lacking the knowledge about the origin of the illness, and the final goal of discovering the actual cure for the disease.

For that reason, we can say that the greatest quality a person needs is not just the willingness to tackle something unknown, but it is the ability to work consistently with unwavering persistence for the length of time required to make a breakthrough in his particular area of research. In other words, a researcher must have faith until he or she masters the knowledge that leads to the achievement of the ultimate goal, which is to find the cure and be able to treat a multitude of people who have this particular illness.

Researcher of the Soul

If we can take our example to a different scale, we can say that a person who desires to believe in something invisible, such as the existence of God, and especially if he or she desires to achieve the capability of communicating with this invisible God directly, he or she must choose a road comparable to the medical researcher and can expect to find much turmoil and many dilemmas along the way.

Indeed, if someone makes a decision that he or she wants to relate to God for the purpose of feeling God's love, the first thing this person has to know is that there is a gap between the starting place, which is like an infant stage in relationship to God, and the place where this person wants to arrive, which is a mature relationship with God. Due to his or her internal desire, this person is usually recognized as being a religious person. But regardless of this designation, this person has to develop the quality of having faith in his or her dream, as well as working hard to find the way to meet that famous invisible God, if indeed this field of discovery was chosen for the sake of finding a solution to a dilemma—to bring an end to the loneliness of the soul.

If this person can achieve such a goal, then the gap between not knowing God and arriving to the point where he or she can communicate with God will be closed. Then this person will be able to give the solution to stop the loneliness of the soul, and stop a multitude of people from destroying their lives, similar to a doctor who gives a cure to re-establish the health of the people. Indeed, if this solution can be achieved, this person will be viewed as a doctor of the soul.

If we examine these two fields, and many others that demand hard work, we have to agree that the people in these fields need a dream, first, and large amounts of faith to achieve their desired goals. The physician's dream is to bring human beings to the place where they can have healthy bodies, which will allow them to feel good by achieving their most desirable state of physical health. In a similar way, the believer's intention in wanting to approach and communicate with God is to create a healthy internal character—emotionally and spiritually—that will allow this individual, as well as humanity, to have pleasing feelings of happiness forever.

However, if in the process of their research the invisible qualities of faith and persistence become shattered, then surely their ultimate goal cannot be achieved. Still, even though the goal of these researchers is not achieved, whether it be for physical healing or spiritual healing, in many cases they can at least bring partial healing according to their level of faith and discovery. In the case of the religious person, even if he cannot find the absolute relationship with God, he can at least find the way to establish a partial relationship with God.

If we observe carefully a person who wants to believe in God and relate with Him directly, this person will surely discover that it is not easy to grasp the identity of the invisible God at first. Due to this deep reality, when we look at specific individuals who have entered the religious field in the hope of discovering and developing a relationship with God, their demeanors show to us that they have experienced tremendous complications through the years and countless difficulties, even though they maintained a constant desire and unwavering faith.

The reason many religious people look strained is because of the intense effort involved in discovering the distinct nature of God, who appears to be so unapproachable. Perhaps the first thing such a person might try to do is to transcend his mundane thoughts and activities in order to enter a place where nothing exists, not even the wind or any other form of energy. In other words, this person would have to rise above the realm of this physical world to a realm of higher thoughts, in order to find the knowledge of the nature of God. One thing is certain, when a researcher of religion tries to find God, this person allows himself to be extremely vulnerable to this world of the unknown, to the point he could might get lost within the realm of thoughts, similar to an asteroid floating in space at the edge of the solar system. And the reason he will allow himself to do this is because he believes this is the place where God lives.

There are many believers who try to maintain their fragile concepts about the identity of their God, and this is the reason they feel so vulnerable in front of the ones who, without any sign of doubt, come to them with the unbearable request, "…Prove your God to me." Because religious people seem to go somewhere away from this Earth to find their God, they many times become defensive when they are faced with someone who demands, "You there, since you believe in God, explain to me something about your famous God."

Both a researcher of religion who begins the journey to prove the existence of his God, and a scientific researcher who takes the road to discover the process to transform the bad health of human beings into good health, may go through immense doubts and difficulties to find the information they desire to find. However, the scientific researcher can more easily pass through the forest of doubt because what he wants to achieve is connected to the physical matter of human beings, and therefore, when someone asks the scientific researcher a question such as, "Show me your cure," he will have a greater chance to say, "This is my cure and this is how I discovered it." Because this person has something tangible, he can more easily escape from the people who wish to make him lose faith in his dream, but this does not mean he did not confront many doubts and have people heckling him along the way.

If you have ever been confronted with this situation, you would agree that this kind of experience is extremely humbling. One thing is sure, after being questioned and harassed and giving some answer, you are left with a miserable feeling, to the point that you feel your whole existence is shrinking, disintegrating into dust.

In spite of our personal belief that we will reach our goal, which may be to find the cure that would physically heal human beings or to find the relationship with the invisible God to cure the loneliness deep in the heart of human beings, if we have not found the absolute remedy to cure people or to find God, in that moment we can only bow our heads and keep silent in front of the people who question us. And later we may question ourselves whether it was a mistake to want to be a doctor or a religious person in the first place.

Being unable to find the perfect answer, especially in the field of religion, no matter how great our explanation can be, we can still find ourselves shrinking when we are confronted with questions. Surely this event will make us feel we have to surrender to the one who looks superior at that time, not because he has a better answer than we do but because the questions he asks are the same ones that we are trying to find the answers for, questions of what God is all about and what kind of relationship humanity can have with this God. Because we cannot explain well or help him experience what we know through our experience, we can observe this person suddenly lifting his head high, with a posture that shows he has achieved a conquest. Then with the superiority of being able to ask what we cannot answer, he will turn his back on us, and we can only bow our heads, feeling we have lost everything.

If this kind of event happens to us, the question we should ask ourselves is, "Did I lose everything, or did I simply lose the opportunity to convey my beliefs to that specific person who asked the questions?"

However, the issue still remains, is there a way for human beings to believe in a God who has the main characteristic of being invisible, and still be able to describe with honor and a sense of persuasion what they believe or know, regardless some people will squeeze them into a place where they feel useless?

If they can take this accusation in a positive way, this event can make them closer to God day by day. And the reason

I say this is because surely God knows that all the people who want to believe in Him will be confronted with the reality of His invisibility and therefore will be vulnerable to those who cannot just believe there is an existence inside the world of invisibility. If we look from God's viewpoint, we can imagine that His greatest desire for human beings, who were initiated by Him and for Him, must have been for them to easily be able to believe in Him, and that He sees their difficulties with much sadness.

Because there are a multitude of obstacles between God and humankind, this difficulty to explain a relationship with God is similar in complexity to trying to explain the relationship between two individual beings or the relationship between our body and our brain. This is why it can sometimes take decades of research for scientists to find an answer, if not more. But regardless it is difficult to find a suitable answer, no doctor or researcher, in the name of knowledge and helping humanity, will quit their research. Likewise for religious people, even thought they may be unable to find a suitable, comprehensible way to explain their relationship with God, nothing within themselves should cause them to quit or stop striving to find a better way to present their explanation.

Matter or Symbol

When religious people are faced with the difficulty of presenting to others what they most highly value, if in that moment they could accept to look at what is happening around their own lives instead of putting on their glasses and delving into their old books, they could perhaps find a more convincing way to prove the existence of that invisible God. For example, if they could visit the backyard of their church, temple or mosque, for sure they would begin to see a multitude of things existing around them, like sweet-smelling flowers, lush plants, and trees so tall that we cannot help but be impressed by them. And by closely observing these delicate flowers, plants and trees, they would find themselves asking, "If God is so invisible, how is it possible He could create a tree that looks visible to our eyes? Why are the trees not invisible like God is invisible? If it is God who created all these things, how did He transform something invisible into something visible?"

Certainly we all know that flowers, plants, and trees are not invisible, at least to our eyes. So what are they? Well, we can say they are made purely of material elements containing a lot of space in between in order for energy to pass through. But we also can ask if nature, so brilliantly displayed all around us, is just composed of matter in the middle of space, or if it can be viewed as many symbolic forms of Someone greater? Are the trees just objects for us to enjoy sitting under when it is too hot and used to make houses, furniture or paper, according to our demands, or are they designed above all to be the symbols of Someone invisible to our eyes?

Surely observing these two views—to see an object as a symbol of Someone invisible or to see an object as a piece of matter in the middle of space—can make us question which one was the original way to see. From a material viewpoint, when we look at a forest of trees we may instinctively ask ourselves what profit we can gain from those trees. But if humans were to quietly ask the One who initiated those trees, "What is their purpose to be there?" maybe we would find a different view, one more related to the field of beauty.

To understand these two completely different views, let's look at someone who considers himself a believer, like a Christian. Such a person will claim to communicate with Jesus or try to achieve that, but if we observe the relationship we might realize that, for whatever reason, he often does not relate directly to Jesus. Instead he will chose a few objects, like a candle which when lit represents the brightness of Jesus, or like incense that symbolizes the eternal life of Jesus, or a cup of wine and bread in association with the physical life of Jesus. Based on his belief in one or all of these chosen objects, he will consider himself to be relating with the person of Jesus.

If we look at these items in a purely secular way, we can say that by themselves they do not have any particular distinction but are objects that are used in daily life. However, based on the thoughts or beliefs connected to these items, they can represent something with an amazingly high value.

To understand this point, maybe some of you have had the opportunity to attend a church service where people valued these objects. If you did, you would have noticed that the cleric spent a significant amount of time focusing on two specific objects. From the biblical story of two thousand years ago we know that Jesus celebrated a ceremonial meal with his friends and disciples, which later came to be known as the Last Supper. According to the story, in the midst of this meal Jesus introduced two objects, which still today after so many centuries are remembered and recognized as the way to be close to the presence of Jesus.

One of those objects is a cup that is used to hold wine and the other object is bread or the 'host'. Individually, the wine is considered to represent the blood of Jesus while the special bread represents the body of Jesus, and together the ceremony is to represent the last supper of their Lord. These two objects used by most Christians are not viewed by them as simply secular items that they could buy and use every day for their meals. Instead, these items are viewed as something those believers wish to receive from the one they long to love.

These two objects, as the story goes, were selected at a specific moment by Jesus himself and were to be used to remember his mission, for the ones who believed in him. This is the reason we can read in the Bible that such a ceremony was to be performed in remembrance of him. And it is interesting that from that time forward, those who believe in Jesus' mission have continued to perform a ceremony of that last meal. Through this ceremony, all the believers of the past as well as today hope ultimately to become one with Jesus. And regardless their main desire through that special ceremony is to follow what the disciples did and try to become one with Christ, many are still longing to receive the substantial, physical Christ, in order to transform themselves from a state of death into a state of life, which is represented as the resurrection.

As is written in the Bible, these objects were originally given to remind the people around Jesus about one final event, which was surely the most surprising moment of that final Passover meal. If we could put ourselves inside this specific moment, we would see Jesus at the table with his disciples taking in his hands some bread, and instead of dipping the bread in olive oil in order to start the meal, Jesus showed it to everyone saying "Take and eat, for this is my body" (Matt. 26:26). Then we would see him raising his cup filled with wine, and instead of saying; "Let us celebrate this week of Passover" and giving some good news about their history as those present surely wished him to do, we could be as shocked as those who were attending that unique meal when Jesus spoke about his impending death and his blood that would be shed, saying "Drink from it, all of you" (Matt. 26:27).

We can surely imagine that the disciples' hearts were focused on the commencement of the Passover meal and its significance in their religion. So when they started to hear Jesus suddenly claiming those two objects to represent something so different than they were originally designed for, such an event must have perplexed the disciples. They must have looked at Jesus in that moment with the view that he was acting in quite a bizarre manner. As they tried to comprehend the meaning of what he was saying in relation to the wine and the bread, surely their enthusiasm to be invited to this unique meal of the year would have suddenly shifted to a state of confusion, no longer knowing if what they were witnessing was something positive or something negative. And because of this, the mood of the feast must have become an atmosphere of speculation on what Jesus was speaking about.

What Kind of Bread and Wine?

What then could be the main point of Jesus suddenly drawing attention to these two items, which were so commonly used by everyone at mealtime? Did those two objects suddenly metamorphasize into different shapes and textures? Surely if we could analyze them with our microscopes we would not find anything special about them. But they became special when they were connected to a situation related to Jesus' life and to the lives of the believers. Similarly, if wine poured during the middle of a meal was suddenly identified as an object that could make people rich the next day, everyone in that room would probably drink a lot of wine and value it because it had the potential to make them wealthy. And if the bread was viewed as something that could make the people fertile, allowing them to have many children, then many people would value that bread and eat a lot of it. So we can see that the value of an object is determined by the thoughts we have toward it.

Maybe in the beginning when Jesus presented the wine and the bread to his disciples as being his blood and his flesh, it was not received as great news. But over the centuries these two objects came to be valued as holy objects because they were connected to the thought that they represented Jesus personally. Therefore in order to maintain this belief, the clergy chose to perform a ceremony similar to the last supper. The people who observed that tradition being performed would view the clergy as holy, and the reason they were viewed as such was that maybe they did become holy in the process of performing these ceremonies so many times and through protecting the holy words of Jesus in connection to these two objects.

Because people started to value what these priests were doing, they became interested in coming close to that table called the Table of the Lord. They felt they should be able to be a part of Jesus' life too, and due to this wish they started to believe that if they could drink the wine or take some bread and eat it, they as well would become holy. But the real miracle of these people who began to believe in the words connected to these two objects was that the effort required to participate in the ceremony placed them in the position of having the right to come to His banquet, if the Lord should come again.

Some of us observing this ceremony might easily say, "Let's forget the thought connected to the wine and the bread and see if there is something special within that wine or bread." If we do so, surely we will find absolutely no element that can strengthen our faith in Jesus, or anything in those two objects that will create the desire to connect to Jesus. Instead we will conclude that the cup containing the wine that Jesus interpreted as his blood is unable to have any effect on us.

And because we humans have the capacity for two categories of thought, one being spiritual and one physical, many who observed this holy ceremony became skeptical toward what the priests were doing. But if these people were sincere, they would admit that when they drank the wine or ate the bread, it was not those two objects that were special, it was the thought connected to them that was special. Therefore if the person did not see the thought as valuable and so removed it, then it is understandable indeed why the wine became just wine and the bread became just food to sustain us for a few hours, nothing more.

But despite some people not valuing the thought behind such objects, there were many who did value the thought behind these objects and could therefore strengthen their faith and obedience toward Jesus. And because of their faith toward Jesus' word, they were permitted, from time to time, to receive a special feeling of closeness with Jesus when they received the two objects during the ceremony identified by them as the Holy Communion. Due to this event, many people who experienced some feeling would remember it for a long time, to the point they would feel they entered the realm of being engaged religiously.

If some could arrive to the place where they could feel communion with Jesus, their feelings and their physical matter could coalesce. But there were others who could not maintain their belief so ardently. As a result, they began to disconnect themselves from the viewpoint that explained how Jesus was related to that cup of wine and that bread. And due to that, instead of being in holy communion with Jesus, they felt excluded from the right to experience the communion, to the point they would eventually question their faith and why they were attending the church service in the first place. Indeed, a person who tries to feel the love of Jesus without having any object that can symbolize Jesus will find it immensely difficult to receive something from him, and may even feel lost spiritually because of having nothing to clearly focus on.

The Value of Thought and Matter

If we go back to the Last Supper and imagine that Jesus did not give any thought toward those objects but just presented them as matter, there would not be any way to communicate with Jesus through those objects. To illustrate this point, we can say that if we go to a restaurant and are served wine and bread, these objects exist without any higher value besides being used to fulfill the needs of our own flesh.

However, to the ones who believe in and focus their attention on the words Jesus gave in connection to these two objects, surely they will have the chance to feel Jesus coming. It is similar if they focus on the words he said, "What you do to others you do to me", and apply them in situations with the people around them. Because of the thought that exists behind the two objects of the Last Supper—'This is my blood and this is my flesh'--the believers could strengthen their faith and direct their minds to Jesus. And at the same time, if a believer could recognize that thought over and over, this effort would create a base in that person that would permit Jesus to approach him very closely. However, if these objects did not have a specific thought connected to them, humanity would never know the value of Jesus, which means he would have become an unknown personage.

If any person has the desire to feel the presence of Jesus, he will first need to know the stories around the physical life of Jesus, about specific objects he touched or people he interacted with. For example, Jesus washed the feet of the disciples with water, to show humility and service. At one time he gave a story about the sparrows—"Not one is forgotten by the Father….Therefore don't be afraid, you are worth more than many sparrows" (Luke 12:6-7). Through valuing Jesus' thought behind each physical object, people can begin to experience deeper feelings toward him. The moment they consciously make the effort both to remember the story about some physical situation and then believe in Jesus' viewpoint toward that situation, they will be able to receive more personal feelings toward Jesus.

We can therefore say that when we look at a physical object that represents our physical aspect and value some thought that represents our spiritual dimension, by viewing these two aspects equally we connect the physical and mental parts of ourselves. This means we are actually unifying within ourselves the visible part, which is our body, with the invisible part, which is our mind. And because of this unity within, we can create a base to receive feelings from God.

Indeed, the love of God through Jesus has been desperately waiting to be transmitted to us. Yet, until believers can find the perfect basis of belief in Jesus' words in relation to the objects of faith he used, this love will have to continue to wait. This difficulty on the part of most believers to associate a thought with the matter explains why so few people experience communion with Christ, in other words, why so few religious people are able to experience the love of Jesus coming within them.

From this explanation we can understand why the main focus of religious people has been to strive to find the truth or the spiritual viewpoint connected to a physical object or situation, which is actually the only way that will allow them to feel God's love or Jesus' love. Similarly, many other groups of thinkers like philosophers or doctors are trying to find how life functions or what kind of physical laws keep us alive, with the hope that through that knowledge, people will elevate the physical standard of their lives. And although it may not be their intention, through their discoveries they are helping humanity be able to value the thought, or internal aspect, in connection with the physical world. This is the reason many people will accept to recognize the existence of God after discovering the secrets of the laws of matter.

To understand this point, we can see that until Jesus initiated the view of drinking the cup of wine in order to remember him, no one around him at that time had considered the cup he drank from as holy or the bread he ate as different from the bread they were eating with him. This situation tells us that if Jesus did not direct people to value a thought in connection to a specific object, all things would be viewed as just material. In the moment Jesus brought forth a specific thought connecting the cup of wine and the bread with himself, the dimension of something secular or material was elevated to a place of divinity and holiness.

If today we try to understand the reason religions could have been created, we can say that one of the main reasons was to help human beings discover the invisible world of thought, which could be God's thought that brought about this physical world we can see and touch. If the view did not exist that God is the One who created the physical world for the purpose of beauty and love, then human beings would only perceive things based on matter. This absence of knowledge would prevent human beings from understanding and appreciating the full dimension of the created world. But the most dramatic situation is that human beings would not be enabled to enter the realm of feeling, and this would certainly affect their attitudes toward all things around them. When people cannot perceive the dimension of feeling, surely the way they relate with matter becomes more destructive than elegant.

Matter vs. Spirit

If there are some people who are interested in knowing God, it is because something tells them there must be a way to understand this mysterious God, and due to this perception, they feel responsible to find the internal thought behind matter, from the viewpoint of the Creator.

Yet as we know, due to God's nature being invisible, it is easy for human beings to make Him disappear by just creating a few thoughts, like, "Human beings can control matter" or "Matter exists based on matter", rather than connecting what is visible to our Creator and seeing visible things as symbols of Him. Regardless human beings have the tendency to want to dismiss the thoughts that are connected to value and purpose when we see a visible object, one thing we do not understand is that in dismissing the internal thought, something else disappears as well, which is the feeling that is supposed to accompany this object.

What about more religious-oriented people? We often find that religious people focus on the spiritual realm to an extreme, only valuing thoughts referring to God without connecting those thoughts to physical matter or to human beings. Interestingly, these people will find the same result as those who remove the value of the thought connected to matter. This means, by considering matter as having little value and not recognizing it as important, and only valuing their belief because it represents the spirit, religious people will also find it impossible to receive any feeling from the word, regardless they consider the word as coming 'from God'.

Most of the time those people who carry religious beliefs will be confronted and rejected by those who believe in materialism or atheism. As a result, the religious person and the atheist will find themselves disconnecting from each other and eventually fighting against each other in the hope of making their beliefs dominant over the other. Due to their extreme positions of being the protectors of their viewpoint, we can see throughout history the constant struggle between two major groups of ideas: the belief that the word is more important than physical matter, and the view that physical matter is more important than religious beliefs. This struggle can translate into a fight over whether the physical life of today is more important than the spiritual life of tomorrow, which many consider to be Heaven.

If we observe the religious people, it is common to see them emphasizing only the invisible or 'spiritual' aspect behind everything. Therefore, it is understandable that because of this extreme view, many people who believe in the material world and the teachings of science will choose to reject religion as being too spiritual and not scientific enough.

At the same time, those who consider themselves to be religious critique the people who believe matter to be the most important part of their daily lives. As a result of seeing materialism to an extreme degree, some religious people take the road of rejecting material things and may become afraid to even speak, for instance, about the good taste of food or afraid to gain wealth from this world.

We can see the dilemma that each group has concerning the other group as a result of the extremity of their views. And yet we can question, how can one prove the validity of a thought whose nature is primarily invisible, without connecting that thought to matter? And as well, how can one value matter if one rejects the thought that could have caused it to come into existence?

This quandary about the value of what is spiritual and what is physical, or what is 'God' and what is 'not God', did not begin with human beings. This struggle must have begun before human beings were created, especially if we suppose the nature of God is to be invisible. If God knows what kind of substance He is made of, surely He must have been thinking how He would be able to make Himself known to humanity. And we can believe He must have been desperate to find the way to make Himself recognized by human beings, long before He ever began to develop the physical creation.

So we can say that God and humanity are trying to discover how to reach one another, knowing God is extremely invisible while human beings appear to be extremely physical. And because of this constant effort coming from both sides, there is hope that one day we will begin to be able to communicate with one another.

The Origin of the Physical World

We know there are many ideas concerning the origin of this physical world. Scientists have been trying to discover the answer to this mystery through long years of research. But, regardless of the different theories we have come up with as answers to how and why we were created, it would perhaps be more appropriate for us to address our questions to God and ask Him directly, why did He create this visible, physical world? Since He is the One who initiated this whole thing, He is the One who must know why. But regardless He must know why, since human beings have immense difficulty to elevate themselves to a position of oneness with God, they also have immense difficulty to find His viewpoint. And if some humans are able sometimes to hear Him speaking, there are many who believe those thoughts could not have come from God but must have come from the imagination of the person.

Indeed, many religious people have tried to find the viewpoint of God, but because they mix vertical and humanistic thoughts inside their minds, many of their ideas contain seemingly contradictory suggestions. Some think that everything in the creation came about by the grace of God in a matter of a very short time, because someone recorded that creation took a mere seven days, while other religious people believe that the 'seven days' could be symbolic of a much longer process of creation. These contractions impel many scientists to come up with the theory that everything came into existence for purely physical and biological reasons. But, regardless their scientific discoveries show the creation process could have taken more time, this material viewpoint clearly does not satisfy the inner aspect of human beings.

As a result, many find themselves rebelling against any explanation that we are made solely biologically or solely spiritually. The reason we have difficulty to accept either explanation as an absolute answer is because human beings are not made with only an external aspect but with an inner aspect as well. In other words, human beings are not made only according to the laws of science but are also made according to the Word, which is meant to direct our level of goodness.

Surely it is difficult for people who are educated in using scientific methods to be able to work with and relate to things they cannot perceive by physical means. Therefore if someone were speaking about an idea that necessitated a sense of imagination, they would connect that idea to religious people. From the perspective of matter-oriented people, believers often appear to be interested only in what is happening in the sky or above the clouds, and indeed, many believers seem to consider that what is valuable must not be visible to their eyes or within the touch of their hands.

The gap that has arisen due to these extreme views toward life has caused the formation of two major groups, which only separates humanity instead of uniting it. To overcome this division, some human beings propose that the only way for religion to flourish again is to remove science. Yet surely the scientific people could say that the reason we are separated is because of all these people who believe in abstract and irrational theories, and therefore the only way to make unity is to remove all religious beliefs and educate all humanity about the scientific method. And if someone with this viewpoint of materialism were to gain a position of power, he would probably be thinking about how to achieve his goal of removing religious viewpoints.

If we observe these two groups, they definitely do not have the same interest or focus. Religious people unwaveringly value their belief in the existence of God. By contrast, those interested in science are focusing mainly on understanding the mechanisms of matter, such as what matter consists of and how it functions. And due to that knowledge, scientific people have the tendency to promote the idea that matter arose from matter alone. This means they believe that there is no initiator who could have influenced this matter. In other words, many scientific minded people come to the point where they think it is all right to reject God. But by their rejection of God, we can say they are going beyond the scientific field and toward the territory of invisible belief. Finally, they present themselves as wanting to remove the very One who could have created or initiated all the physical things they enjoy, whom the religious people call 'God'.

Surely if those scientific people would content themselves with trying to understand the mechanisms of matter, the other group would not experience as many feelings of resistance toward them. But we can assume the interests of scientists do not stop with discovering the purely scientific aspects. It appears that they are tempted to express their thoughts of not wanting to agree with the possibility that there is a Creator above matter. Or, the reason they could want to reject the possibility of a Creator is maybe because their scientific discoveries make them feel the authority to believe they can create anything, and due to this they consider they could be equal to God and eventually above God.

On the other hand, we could make the argument that if the group from the realm of science feels tempted to initiate the idea that science exists by science alone or that matter exists by matter alone, maybe it is because religious people have as well disregarded matter as being a vibrant and essential element of life. Due to the negligence of those from the religious world in accepting the laws of science, meaning the physical laws of matter, the door was opened for scientific-minded people to disregard the religious view that the world was initiated by God. To remedy this situation, if religious-minded people can not just look toward the skies but can acknowledge what exists around them as well, they will begin to see that all the created objects—the air, water, soil, plants and animals—can also be viewed as existing in accordance with the laws and principles of God that scientists have uncovered.

The Message Behind the Symbol

If religious minded people could recognize the views of those in the field of science as being valid and at the same time promote the idea that the physical creation serves to help the human mind to perceive the invisible characteristics of the Creator, then perhaps matter would no longer be viewed as merely dust that turns back to dust. Instead, people would begin to perceive that all physical things existing through the laws of science could be viewed as the most holy objects, in whom we can discover the nature of the invisible Creator, God.

Surely if the religious believers reflect upon the story Jesus left with them, they would realize how a simple cup was transformed into holiness by adding a specific thought, giving it the qualification to become a symbol of Jesus. Surely if believers examine this miraculous transformation, they will realize that there is a way to communicate with someone who is invisible, in this case Jesus, by using a physical object as a symbol of that person.

In order to make this view more perceivable, let's create a scenario. I am sure we have all met someone who got inspired to purchase some roses from his local flower shop. Do you think his inspiration came because his house was missing color and he wanted to brighten it up a bit? Or do you think he purchased those flowers to symbolically express the excitement of his heart and show the passion that he carried within for some person?

As we all know, the feelings of the heart are invisible and this reality makes it difficult to express those feelings. Of course we can always express our feelings with words but perhaps this man felt that communicating his feelings through words was too direct and was missing a certain charm. He preferred to explore the realm of symbolic objects as a means to communicate his invisible feelings toward this someone. Fortunately for this gentleman he could find the way to express the feelings within his heart through a bouquet of roses. Indeed, if we look at the immense world of creation, we can see that he could have chosen any category of flower, like tulips, lilies, daffodils, etc.

For just a moment let's compare the situation of this gentleman to what might have happened on the part of God, who has many feelings and wishes to express them. From this viewpoint, it is understandable that if the invisible God wishes to express His feelings for human beings, He will use physical objects to do so. Therefore in order to achieve this, He came up with the idea to create a grandiose physical creation. But what is different between God and the gentleman is that God must have worked hard to come up with the many styles of lovely flowers, the wide assortment of trees and plants, the humungous variety of unique insects, and we could go on and on.

As we see with the young gentleman who wants to express his happiness to someone, God as well felt the best way to communicate His feelings to humanity was through using symbolic objects, instead of through intellectual, invisible words, which people could interpret in many ways.

Of course, if we observe the gentleman who buys flowers, we can look at him in just a purely pragmatic way, and say that he buys flowers because it is part of his weekly routine. But if we take another view, we can imagine that he maybe had an immense quantity of feelings going on inside him and therefore he received the inspiration to buy the bouquet of flowers to represent his feelings. And because of his intentions, he actually increased the value of those flowers, which at first looked purely material.

If we could ask the man, he would say the reason he bought the flowers was because he felt they would express his feelings better than he could through words alone. As someone once said, "A picture is worth a thousand words", therefore based on his wish to communicate a thousand words or more, this gentleman chose to give a big bouquet of red roses.

If the gentleman's main objective in choosing flowers was to express his feelings toward someone through a physical symbolic object, then we can ask the question, did he want to give the flowers simply to reveal his feelings? Or was it also because he was anticipating and hoping that the person to whom he was going to present the bouquet would decode the message he wished to express through it?

If by accident the person who was given this bouquet of roses did not recognize the symbolic meaning behind them, we would not be surprised to see her eventually placing them in some obscure corner of her kitchen. And if this gentleman saw his flowers in some dark corner of the house every time he bought her a fresh bouquet, surely he would start to feel there was a misunderstanding between the two of them. Maybe the man would sense that this lady did not know how to care for flowers. Another thought he could have is that perhaps she didn't know these flowers were given to her as a means of expressing his deep inner feelings. And eventually if he discovered she could not perceive the message, surely this gentleman would begin to question why he should continue to communicate to her through this particular symbol of a bouquet of flowers.

Indeed, out of desperation he might begin to research if there were a school where human beings could learn the language of symbols. In other words, the school he would like to find would be not just a place to analyze physical objects in order to learn how they function, but a place to learn what feeling can be associated with what particular object. Surely if he could find this school, he would ask the lady to go there with the hope that she could discover his feelings for her in relation to the bouquets.

If we have ever had a similar experience, we can realize that unless we learn the thoughts behind symbols, we will always be sitting on the edge of fragile relationships. If we do not understand the message behind the symbol, we will be unable to perceive the heart of the person who sent the symbol, regardless we receive the secular object. Instead of looking at each other mutely, wishing to express what we feel but unable to make sounds with our voices, and feeling sad and frustrated, if indeed we could find a school to learn symbolic expressions in connection to our thoughts and feelings, we would surely be able to improve the relationships between human beings.

God Wishes to Communicate Through the Physical World

If we have ever experienced this difficulty of wishing to communicate a deep feeling through a physical object and not being understood, we might also understand how there can be much frustration on the part of God's heart, because He has such a mass of feelings to express. We can therefore understand why He would create the whole symbolic system of expression, where feelings can be understood through physical objects. Based on observing what a wide variety of objects exist in the world around us, we could discover how vast the invisible heart of God can be.

But regardless to God the meaning behind a tulip, a frog or a puppy is clear, since He knows what feelings He had when He created them, there is still something He had to figure out after human beings were created. He had to find a way to educate human beings to understand the meaning of these objects, knowing they were not with Him when He created all things. And surely God must have mixed feelings when He sees human beings sitting in front His world of symbols, as we do many times in the park when we look at the flowers, the trees and squirrels, etc. with nothing in our minds, barely even recognizing their beauty. Surely God must be wondering if we humans understand the reason why such symbols were created. Based on this situation of God who wishes to relate with humans, or the gentleman with his lady, we can say that maybe we also treat the flowers and other things in creation as the lady in our story treated the bouquet of roses the man presented to her.

Surely if we are sincere when we stroll through a garden with its dozens of varieties of flowers, we have some sense that these wonderful colors and smells do not exist strictly for the sake of our survival or even merely to entertain our eyes. This means that humans can view the garden through a dimension other than just the physical dimension, and realize that these flowers are an expression of the beauty of someone. Also, as humans, we can recognize through the styles and arrangements of the flowers within the garden that they are an expression of the landscape gardener, regardless he or she may not be present at that moment.

If the garden arrangement is an expression of the mind and intentions of the one who designed it, the next step is not so difficult, which is to accept that the flowers with their many colors and smells and the numerous trees and animals living in the garden can all be expressions of God's feelings, as well. In other words, like the mind of the landscape designer is part of the beauty of the garden, we also can acknowledge that the entire garden can be a symbol of the mind of the invisible God.

The Whole World Can Become Holy

What do you think would happen if you were to elevate your mind to the viewpoint of seeing flowers as symbols of God's heart? Surely you would feel that the entire Earth could suddenly be Heaven. In other words, this land that we often refer to as Mother Earth could be recognized as a divine Mother Earth, instead of just a material Earth.

If we can believe in the concept that when we see magnificent flowers we are seeing the magnificence of God, surely we are going to experience another dimension, or another realm of energy. But if we look at a garden just as a plot of dirt filled with sparkles of color manifesting themselves through chemical reactions of magnesium and oxygen, we will surely be unable to experience this higher dimension of energy.

Knowing this, if we now can take a trip through any park on a beautiful sunny day and connect the physical objects we see around us with a divine origin, we can maybe better understand why people who call themselves religious perceive an item such as a cup, a book, a candle, or a bell as a holy symbol of the Almighty God.

Although it is interesting to see religious people choosing certain objects to represent the holiness of their leaders or their God, if we deeply observe the created world around us, we can recognize how many things God created as holy compared to how many things human beings consider as holy. And we might be quite shocked to realize the gap, because the multitude of objects God created as expressions of His heart is so enormous that we can question if perhaps human beings do not want to experience holiness.

Imagine if the people who celebrate and honor the two objects of the cup of wine and the bread as symbols of their Lord and God—if they would take a moment before beginning their ceremony to slowly walk around the garden surrounding their church. Surely with each step they would see a new assortment of flowers, and if a soft breeze were to pass in that moment, they might catch beautiful aromas coming from those flowers, bringing great pleasure to their noses as well as to their eyes.

After such an experience, their thoughts might start to deepen to contemplate the symbolic messages these flowers were trying present to them, through such pleasant aromas and sparking colors. And with time they might even discover the invisible nature of God's heart, as they make the connection between the objects they are seeing and the thought of what these objects might have been created to express. Surely if the people on the way to attend their holy service or meeting would first tour the flower beds and shrubbery that surround their place of worship, upon entering their building they would realize that they carried the perfume of the flowers upon their clothes. And this realization could make their God happy, because He could believe the people came to make communion after learning how to see Him.

If all of us would adopt this new viewpoint of seeing all the creation existing around us as symbols of God's love, then religious people—who have the tendency to choose a few objects—would feel the need to be more open and to welcome many objects as resembling the divinity of God. Maybe, for better or for worse, this new view of looking at the creation as a divine expression of God would no longer permit the priests or ministers to view themselves and their religions as unique or special. Instead this viewpoint would make them truly ecumenical, because in the moment we view everything existing around us as not purely material but as expressions of the Creator's feelings or heart, the need to come to a specific building to meet God will be brought into question. Instead, this new awareness would allow people to expand their opportunities to meet and to experience God in many other places, if they were interested in doing so.

If we return to the experience of the gentleman who tried to make himself understood by presenting a bouquet of flowers to his lady, we can realize no matter how many times he offered bouquets of different arrangements or maybe even a wagonful of flowers, as long as that lady continued to not comprehend what the flowers were meant to transmit internally, she would maybe enjoy the physical flowers but still not understand the emotional intent of the gentleman's heart. And because of her incomprehension of the deeper meaning of those bouquets, she might barely utter a 'thank you', and perhaps even wonder why he was bringing these flowers.

Based on this dilemma, in order to relate to each other and with God, we can say indeed that if humans do not elevate and grow their knowledge, they cannot develop themselves in the dimension of feeling. Instead, if we can accept to believe that the reason there is such an assortment of flowers and trees growing all around us is not simply to remove the monotony of the landscape, but is as well to discover the heart of Someone who has the characteristic of being invisible, whom we call God, then this time we are not only elevating our minds but are entering inside the dimension of love.

If we can see this way, then the next time someone gives us a beautiful bouquet of flowers, we will understand that we are meant not only to enjoy its beauty visually and aromatically, but we should experience the emotional expression of the one who gave it, as well. And if we can have this view when we walk through a garden observing the abundance of magnificent creation within it, then instead of feeling far away from God, in that moment we can realize that we are indeed living next to Him.

Similarly, if the lady who does not understand why the gentleman gives her these floral bouquets were to ask the owner of the flower shop why people buy flowers, surely that shopkeeper would be able to provide as many as 21 or even 210 reasons why people come to buy flowers. This profusion of explanations from his part explains why many flower shops are so busy, due to people who want to buy flowers for so many occasions.

Therefore, a flower shop would be the perfect place for this lady to learn about the intentions people have in buying flowers and offering them to someone. After this education at the flower shop, if that gentleman were to come again to bring her a bouquet of roses, this time she would know how to take care of those flowers and at the same time would understand that gentleman for the first time.

In a similar manner, if we who receive all these things that are spread around our lives can start to recognize them as more than just physical objects, we will find ourselves altering our attitude toward God, as He will also do toward us. We will find ourselves with a way to approach God, and we will be so grateful, especially if we recall the time when we were young and our hearts were calling us to have a relationship with the God we heard about from our elders. We may remember how many dilemmas we experienced concerning what to say to that God, and when, after finding ourselves not knowing what to say to God, we may have come to the conclusion that it was impossible to communicate with Him. Certainly, this must have been truly a miserable conclusion for God to hear from our lips.

Now, we can realize that one of the major reasons we find ourselves concluding that it is impossible to relate with God is because the words we say to God generally have nothing to do with His character. But if we try to talk to God about the things that interest Him, things He loves and created, surely these thoughts will reach Him. If we can train ourselves to see God's nature through all the many physical things found within numerous places, environments and situations, we will find ourselves having interesting and positive things to say to Him, which will captivate Him and eventually elicit a response. And as we find ourselves able to recognize His nature in people, our relationship with God will grow even deeper.

Similarly, if the woman who now understands the significance of a bouquet of flowers starts to speak about the pleasure those flowers give to her, surely that will open the heart of the man. At the same time, she will see the miracle of her heart opening as well, when she expresses this understanding. Suddenly their conversations can progress to the next sphere, which is the invisible feelings of the gentleman, and as the conversation unfolds, the gentleman may find himself expressing his feelings for her in words. As the lady listens to what the gentleman has to say, she might begin to experience the magic of his feelings coming inside her, and she will perhaps begin to express something back to him, and from here we can see the beginnings of a relationship evolving.

By the lady receiving the knowledge of what can be represented by a gift of roses, she will actually open the realm of relationship, which is composed of feelings. In a similar manner, if human beings start to understand the deeper meaning of why such assortments of flowers, trees, animals, and especially people, were created, we can begin the process of discovering the intentions of God. Little by little we will appreciate His heart and surely that will have an effect upon our own hearts. The more we identify what we feel and share our discoveries with God, the more our emotions will start to accelerate toward Him and expand within us.

A New Way to See God

Certainly, if anyone decides to look at the flowers and plants in a garden as being symbolic aspects of God, instead of just physical objects composed of the chemical and biological building blocks of matter, this person will begin to perceive and feel the presence of God more and more often. Many people teach a complex concept of God and the kind of ceremonies we need to perform in order to communicate with Him or for Him to communicate with us. But the moment we choose a divine thought and direct it toward every physical object, we will create a duality and a base that allows us to feel the presence of the eternal Being.

To illustrate this idea we can look at a cactus as an example. If God created the cactus, He must have known there would be some human being who would love it, regardless its design does not allow it to be so approachable. And if someone is able to see this cactus as a symbol of some part of God's character, that cactus will surely assist him or her in meeting some aspect of God.

After cultivating our minds to see all objects in the environment where we live daily as expressions of God instead of matter alone, when we go back inside those houses of worship to celebrate the mass or the service, we would not have difficulty putting a particular thought of divinity behind specific objects, like seeing the cup of wine as symbolizing the blood of Jesus or the unleavened bread as His holy flesh. Through this effort of matching the thought with the matter, we can also understand, in the reverse, that if people begin to lose or disvalue the divine thoughts connected to their specific objects, this will cause them to separate themselves from those objects.

However, if religious people begin to view other objects of creation with the divine thoughts they practice within their houses of worship, they will realize these thoughts can be used toward every part of their lives. And the more they learn from science how intricately objects are created, the more natural it will be for them to believe the flowers, the trees and the rocks are symbols of the feelings and characteristics of God. With this awareness, the entire congregation attending worship would surely prefer to stroll in the park, which they now consider to be the Garden of God, instead of staying inside the building referred to as the House of God.

We know in the time that we are currently living we often hear young people express how they feel uncomfortable and sometimes strange when they are called to attend the religious services of their parents. One of the main reasons is because they cannot relate when they see their parents focusing their thoughts or attention toward one cup of wine and one small piece of unleavened bread. Many times they become even more perplexed when they are told that this ceremony is the only way to experience God, because it is difficult for them to accept the logic or the spirituality of this idea.

But if we observe these same young ones walking in a garden, running in a park, swimming in the ocean, or rock climbing in the mountains, we can see their attitude is very different in comparison to when they are attending the ceremonies of their elders. Instead of being static and rigid as their parents are in front of God, most of these young ones want to experience the physical environment to its fullest in order to become part of the emotion of God.

Therefore the experience of climbing a mountain can be not just for the sake of walking on top of high rocks, but for the purpose of breathing and feeling the energy of God. So if young people are no longer coming to the ceremonies that have been passed on from generation to generation since the time of the Last Supper, it does not necessarily mean they are losing God. Instead they are perhaps discovering the original plan God had intended as a way for humans to know Him, before people ever began creating temples and cathedrals.

If we, too, amble from rock to rock, tree to tree, or mountain to mountain, with the view that we are walking on top of a holy planet, surely in the end we will not want to walk on a simple ant that is working hard for its survival. Instead we will take a moment to sidestep that ant so it can continue to fulfill its destiny. And by taking this path, we will discover that this whole planet is designed by God so we can perceive His emotion, as well as to acquire a great chance to become holy like Him.

At the end of such a journey God will not see us the same way as when we began. As well, the people living around us will gather close to us and inquire, "You must have discovered a secret." And they will comment, "I remember when you left on your journey and after a few years I can see that you are absolutely transformed and full of light."

From this new viewpoint, every time we see a young person going to a park, the woods, or to visit some other aspect of this wide creation, we should be aware that they are not just trying to escape from the wish of religious people. Instead they are actually learning to be in natural communion with God's love, like many of the people who chose the solitary life of a hermit in order to fulfill their deep desire to discover an intimate relationship between themselves and the invisible God.

However, it is important for young people to remember that many of the objects they encounter were initiated by God in order that they could discover Him through these symbolic forms. With this viewpoint, the creation around them will not just be a piece of land, but all of the creation will be a Holy Land. By adding this divine thought to all they see, these young people will not feel empty but they will begin to fill up their souls with love.

History of Religions

Surely when God was creating the universe, He must not have been content to just observe the creation of our planet and say, "It is good." Knowing God's invisibility, we can say that what He really needed was someone who could relate with His characteristics, which mainly consist of emotion. Regardless He can value His creation, He must have passed through many thoughts concerning how He could create something to not just live on Earth and die, but a being who could learn to relate with Him during its time on the Earth, with the hope that He could have someone to relate with in the time beyond this physical realm.

To achieve this goal, God made human beings capable of creating ideas in order to relate with Him at least intellectually. This is the reason human beings have the tendency to strive to discover the mechanisms of the physical world. Regardless God knew human beings would eventually discover His secrets of how things in this physical world are created, He was hoping, in the midst of these discoveries, that human beings would discover the knowledge necessary to find Him, even though nothing physically proves His existence besides the immense creativity and the principles that allow this wide creation to live in harmony.

Although the physical world has so much diversity, unless human beings can find the connection between God's motivation for creating it and their own internal characters, they will always look at the physical world as being purely material, and because of this they will view themselves that way too.

To remedy the tendency of human beings to focus on knowledge connected primarily to the secular realm, some people became interested in finding God, and because of that the birth of religions began. Through the focus of these religious people who were many times suffering for their faith, there were 'breakthroughs' on different levels that permitted human knowledge in relation to God to become more comprehensive. When a religion person could discover specific divine thoughts in connection to specific physical objects, this person could begin to feel the presence of God, and surely God would be happy to know this person. Through practicing various rituals in connection to these thoughts, this person together with others could begin to attract the heart of God.

Therefore, because someone discovered, to some degree, the secret to meeting the feelings of God, eventually a group of people decided to dedicate a specific day for performing a specific ceremony in order to meet God, which permitted people one day when they did not need to work on their land. On that day everyone stopped being concerned about their physical survival and instead chose to go to their respective houses of worship where divine thoughts could be connected to symbolic objects, so that human beings could be able to catch a glimpse of the world of emotion.

In religions we find the genesis of the idea to connect a divine thought to a physical object. However, if we begin to view the entire created world around us as symbols of God, God will be free to approach us not only in specific moments or places, but at any time of the day or week. If humans can perceive this secret way to see life, surely the purpose of religion has been accomplished, because all people will advance to the stage of being able to acknowledge the wonderful creation around them as the symbols of God. Through this elevation of our thought, God will be able to see human beings not just as servants but as His own children, which we can imagine will give greater joy to Him, and to us as well.

Now we can understand why God would take millions of years to create this world, not just because it takes that long to create plants and animals but because God wanted to make sure His character would be visible through these plants, flowers, trees, and animals. God knew that if human beings could not see His irresistible beauty printed within the characteristics of the creation, they would never perceive the beauty of His loving heart.

In addition to observing the beauty of this environment, we can also begin to understand that God created human beings in a very distinct way in comparison to the world of animals and plants. What is unique about human beings is that He placed in them the ability to recognize how the creation is made, as well as the ability to recognize the invisible God through all things existing in the physical environment. Because of this, God knew that if human beings could educate themselves to recognize that the physical world was created to express His nature, this would allow the human race to realize their full capacity by increasing their senses and thus welcoming the presence of God within them.

If we accept to educate ourselves with divine thought in relation to matter, our senses will open immensely. Then when we visit a park, we will realize that everything has been made for us to see and perceive the invisible characteristics of God. Through the wide array of plants and animals, the wide range of sounds coming from the creation around us, and the smell of the many fragrances, we will realize that all these things were made in order for us to admire Him, to adore Him, and to love Him as the origin.

Jesus as the Symbol of God

Based on discovering that there is a way for human beings to relate with God, we can question if there could be someone who, through practicing this way, became one with God or became the image of God? Surely, this question must have come to many religious people who themselves tried to have a breakthrough in their relationship with God. And because of the difficulty to have this kind of breakthrough, it seems logical that anyone who wants to practice this path of linking a particular thought with a physical object in order to meet the invisible God will surely be happy to know that someone has already fulfilled this quest, instead of considering he or she is the first one to begin this journey.

Interestingly, throughout long periods of history, we have heard of some individuals who could achieve this special relationship with God. Usually we call such an individual a prophet or a master, or some other respectful name according to the popular language of the time. And if we can feel some comfort to know there have already been some who could arrive to a place of oneness with God, we can believe that God must have been very happy to find those individuals as well. And based on this achievement, some prophets were elevated to the position of Beloved Son of God. The historical record shows at least one person who achieved this unique relationship with the invisible God, who was called Joshua or Yeshua or Jesus.

As mentioned before, we know that Jesus, at the end of his life, presented to his disciples a cup of wine and a piece of unleavened bread, and said they were to be used as symbols to remember him. Although this event has been regarded as the greatest event that ever took place, in fact this event only provides a clue to the mission Jesus wanted to accomplish but was unable to.

When Jesus inaugurated these two objects as symbols of himself, surely God must have been traumatically saddened, because He knew that if His beloved Son used objects other than himself to represent him or his mission, it meant the people around Jesus must have been having immense difficulty believing in him as a physical person who was carrying God's love. Jesus knew he must salvage something from this terrible situation of people not wanting to believe that he was the substantial embodiment of God's love. Therefore he had to figure out a way to at least give them a thought connecting a few objects that the disciples were familiar with, like something from the table where they were feasting that very day, with Jesus' divinity. Jesus' intention in choosing these objects was to help the disciples remember Jesus and his mission more than the objects themselves.

In that moment when Jesus was looking for objects to symbolize his mission and himself during that Passover supper, he must have felt miserable, as did his Father in Heaven, regardless this event has been considered to be glorious by people who never saw him, like Paul. Jesus knew that if he was choosing some objects to symbolize himself, it meant that he would soon be removed from the physical realm. In other words, he sensed that some violent event would remove his flesh from this Earth.

Therefore we can understand why Jesus would be sad in that moment, because he had been trying desperately through the years to make his disciples believe he was the physical manifestation of the love of God on Earth. Even though they received words directly from God, like—"This is My Beloved Son"—they had trouble maintaining this viewpoint toward the man they saw physically on Earth.

Due to this difficult situation, Jesus had to choose symbols, something more static, in order to help the disciples believe in the value of the words associated with those symbolic objects. This is why he spoke about the bread and the cup, saying "Take and eat; this is my body" and "Drink from it, all of you. This is my blood of the covenant…" (Matt. 26:26-28). In other words, Jesus was saying that the bread and the wine were characteristics of him, representing masculine and feminine aspects, and if they believed in them they could remove some part of their sin.

The event of Jesus having to choose two secular symbols like the loaf of bread and the cup of wine, viewed today by many as being the most divine moment in history, may have on the contrary been one of the most tragic moments of history from God's viewpoint. And the reason we can make this statement is that God Himself created the whole Earth with all its diversity, in order for human beings to know Him, to see Him and to relate with Him. Ultimately His plan was for humans to be able to receive His love and to fulfill their original destinies of becoming the full manifestations of His love, as Jesus had become.

Therefore, it is hard to imagine that God's beloved Son needed to be destroyed and replaced by two little objects as a remembrance of the Son's hard work, in order for humanity to be saved through their belief in those objects. Surely if we consider Jesus' life as the hope for all on Earth and also consider it is hopeful to have him removed before he could be glorified, it is a similar situation to an architect who is in the process of constructing a five star hotel, and before its completion the workers destroy the hotel. Surely this situation would cause much debate between people, especially if they are logical. But regardless many people must have discussed about why Jesus had to die, the conclusion of this strange debate is that many people consider that Jesus had to be destroyed in order for them to remember his divinity, for the sake of the salvation of humanity. If we consider this idea to be true, then it looks like whatever God creates, we as human beings have to destroy it, in order for us to gain salvation. But we can sincerely question, who really gains salvation? The one who destroys what God creates or the one who glorifies what God creates?

What was God's purpose in building the character of Jesus as His Son on this Earth? Surely if we want to find the answer, we should question what relationship we as the human race should have with Jesus in order for us to be able to achieve our destiny. What was the intention of God in raising up one human being like Jesus at the time when the disciples were around him? Was it to help them to believe that a physical person could become the embodiment of God's love? And could it also be to help the disciples believe that they could become divine beings like Jesus in order to relate with him as adults, instead of as children or servants? If the purpose of believing in Jesus was to help us develop our good character, then destroying Jesus and choosing some symbols to replace Him does not look reasonable or of any great help toward that purpose.

If we consider Jesus was created in order to help us develop our character so we could have a way to relate with God and with Jesus, we can understand as well God's intention in creating everything on this Earth was to help people to relate with Him. But regardless of His intention, it appears that something must have occurred that damaged human beings, causing them to become isolated from that understanding of the value of this physical world in relation to God. Due to this rupture, human beings started to use the creation solely for their own physical survival and personal pleasure, and became incapable of seeing through matter to the invisible side, which was waiting just behind to be discovered.

Even the disciples who were in the presence of Jesus every day could not look at his body and keep the words they had received from God about his divinity, meaning they were quite materialistic. If the disciples were focusing more on the matter than on the value of the word of God, it is understandable why Jesus had great difficulty in making them believe who he really was, not just seeing his body alone but believing in the divine thought associated with his body. That is why he asked the question, "Who do you say I am?" (Matt. 16:15). And regardless in that moment some disciple may have answered that Jesus was the Son of God, which means they did receive a thought from God in connection to Jesus, it look like their real difficulty was that they could not maintain that thought in the midst of their everyday lives.

For example, Jesus asked, "Don't you know me, Philip, even after I have been among you such a long time? Anyone who has seen me has seen the Father. How can you say, 'Show us the Father'?" (John 14:9). If the disciples were able to maintain the thought that God gave to them about Jesus, surely the disciples would not question Jesus as they did. To remedy this event, Jesus gave physical symbols because he understood that in order to receive God's love or energy, we have to make duality with an object and a thought. To help them learn, he chose a familiar object to form one pole and a thought as the other pole. For example, Jesus identified himself as the true vine and the followers as the branches—"I am the vine; you are the branches" (John 15:5)—where the vine is the visible object and Jesus' divinity is the invisible word. If they could connect this symbol with Jesus, they could have realized that they had to become the branches of this vine, meaning to engraft onto Jesus. Jesus knew that God would be able to manifest Himself to them if they could understand his position towards them.

But it looks like regardless how much Jesus tried to help them understand, nothing worked, or if it did work it was just for a short time. Tragically, Jesus could not use every object or symbol that he wanted from his Father's creation to help people remember him. Instead, he was constrained to choose a few objects that were familiar to the disciples, in the hope they could begin to understand his mission through these objects, regardless some of them complained to Jesus about why he spoke in this fashion.

Characteristics of God

If we look at history, we can observe that religious people often share similar concepts. Many use some specific object to symbolize the God they do not see. Some use dramatic symbols like colossal statues of human beings. Others use a simple star, or the sun, the moon, even a flower as their object to symbolize God. But regardless what symbols they use to develop their religions, we can say the main purpose of these symbols was to help human beings remember there is a God somewhere above them in the sky, or even inside of them.

The major thing that has made religions different from one another is what objects they use as a reference for their God. And what has defined religious people from non-religious people has been that those who consider themselves religious have a few specific beliefs behind their chosen objects, whereas other people whom we consider to not be religious have no specific thoughts in connection to the universe or to physical objects. Instead they value objects based on their practicality and usefulness and because of this viewpoint we often categorize these people as being materialistic or atheistic.

Many religions make use of physical objects to symbolize their God, but still we can question why human beings do not choose other branches of the natural world such as plants, flowers, trees, or mountains as symbolic aspects of God, knowing the value and beauty of this creation which has been in the midst of us for so many millions of years. How is it possible that human beings have not yet discovered that whatever was created in the physical world was created for us to see the characteristics of God?

Interestingly, if we look at these two groups of people, we can say that the group that considers all creation solely made of matter seems to have captured the most universally accepted viewpoint. And the reason this viewpoint looks more acceptable to human beings is because it is easier to not choose an internal thought toward all material things.

Now if we observe the group that chooses to have a thought behind the material object, we realize the difficulty is to find a thought that can give value to every object they see. Due to this, they often choose to value just a few objects in the midst of all of the creation as being representations of God. Since each sect or denomination views a few specific objects as holy, they have the tendency to separate themselves from other sects and denominations who value different objects as holy, and this creates a great obstacle to finding a unified base that could help all people accept the realm of divine thought in order to elevate their perception of matter.

If we observe the world of religious people, who hope to see the secular world in a deeper way than the materialistic people do, what they are trying to achieve does not look so complicated if they would only accept to forgo their insistence on being different. If they consider that they have to be in opposition to other groups in order to show that their beliefs are unique, indeed they have achieved this. But because each individual group of religious people has the tendency to only value the thought they have received without looking at what another group has discovered, the world of religious people continues to separate themselves from each other. Furthermore, this deep division among the religions helps the atheist groups to refuse to believe that anything they see physically can be the symbol of the invisible characteristics of God. They know that if this is true, they will have to surrender to

God, which they don't want to be called to do. Regardless of the effects of their divisions, most religious people do not see the need to broaden the thought of their religion, since they believe it comes from God.

In spite of the absence of unity among individual groups of religions, we can see that religious people as a whole do have the tendency to conduct their life differently from people who do not have any beliefs in connection to matter. Due to the matching of thought with matter, religious people have discovered that when they keep certain thoughts toward an object, their feelings of agitation change to calmness, and their feelings of anger can turn into a more respectful attitude. Globally, the groups who believe that a physical object can represent God have the tendency to sense they don't just live on Earth and turn back to dust when they die, but believe that what they build within themselves will exist after their material life is finished. So regardless their view is not yet universal because they don't view everything around them as being holy, they have at least discovered the miracle of seeing a few objects as holy and therefore have opened the way to teach others the value of this view.

On the other hand, the groups who see matter as only being matter continue to experience a multitude of agitated feelings within themselves. Regardless their view toward matter looks quite peaceful and egalitarian, their feelings toward others and toward their environment is sometimes the opposite of peaceful.

Horizontal and Vertical Lines

Let's examine more deeply what happens to us when we attach a thought to a physical object. The moment we remember to connect a view toward a physical object, whether it is a flower, a tree or any other part of this magnificent creation, we are actually forming in that moment a horizontal line between that particular object and ourselves. Due to this, every time we go to the park or go shopping or window-shopping and acknowledge the beauty or the creativity of the objects we see in relation to ourselves, we are actually creating horizontal lines, and these lines will produce certain quantities of energy in us.

However, if we can connect ourselves and the objects we see with the view of acknowledging God at the same time, we are making the base necessary to receive another form of energy, which is vertical energy this time. Through this process, we are actually making the proper alignment within our minds that allows us to receive love from God, which every human being so much yearns to receive. If we can receive this higher, vertical energy, this will allow us to feel less tired than if we see everything purely horizontally or materialistically.

The group whose tendency is to acknowledge just the material aspect has been creating the horizontal line toward all things. And if we study the other group who has the tendency to choose an object in connection to God, we can say they have learned the vertical line. Based on these two groups, one who discovered the horizontal line and the other who discovered the vertical line, we can say that if the two lines are separate from each other, humans will limit the amount of energy they are able to receive and which they so dearly need. But if we can embrace the view we call 'vertical' with the 'horizontal' view, as well, we will be able to receive a higher energy. By making these alignments, each individual person connects to the physical object they have chosen to see, and at the same time connects in some degree to the vertical alignment with God. If we can achieve these alignments repeatedly, over time we will receive a certain amount of energy, which we call love, and if this love can accrue within our soul, this will have the power to transform our character.

If we could observe what we are creating by using both the horizontal and the vertical view, we might realize that we are actually forming a triangle, which has a certain surface area. By creating the form of a triangle around ourselves, we are able to receive the most energy. Based on this knowledge, surely we can understand that if some choose just the horizontal viewpoint, or if some choose just the vertical viewpoint, these people will not receive so much energy.

To understand the difference between a vertical line and a horizontal line, we can say that when we purchase certain items from a shop, if we take the view that they belong only to us because they please us, then regardless we feel happy to choose them, by doing this we are actually only achieving a horizontal line. Due to that choice, we can only receive a small amount of energy from the objects purchased. And as a measurement of how little that energy can be, we will quickly perceive the items we purchased becoming unattractive to us, even after a few short hours or days.

Unfortunately, we usually look at objects without the vertical view. This is because we have not known God's viewpoint in connection to the material world that exists all around us. Perhaps we comment positively about the things we see, recognizing their beauty or wishing to know more about those objects, but this is only creating horizontal lines. Because we do not connect the intention of the Creator with our recognition of the objects we see, we are actually blocking ourselves from receiving His love. Regardless we are maybe in the right place horizontally, because we are not making the vertical line with God, we can only consider that all aspects of the creation are simply material objects having no higher purpose. Due to the lack of thought connecting these objects with God, we cannot experience His vertical love coming down to us. Therefore the life we live on Earth does not stimulate the growth of our hearts because we cannot receive God's love.

Jesus Wanted People to Find the Vertical Line

This idea of the vertical line is maybe not easy for human beings to learn when we have been educated to see everything around us as only physical matter. And knowing the difficulty humans have to recognize just simple objects like trees, stones or birds as symbols of God, how much more difficult it will be for us to recognize a physical person as a symbol of God.

If we make effort to establish the vertical line above the horizontal line, which means we also make a decision to walk the path that Jesus walked, we will become aware of the multitude of difficulties he would have faced when he found himself obliged to help the people to recognize him, not as a human being because everybody knew he was a physical human being, but to recognize that he came as the living embodiment of God's love. Since we know there are so few people who focus on building these two lines, we can imagine that those around Jesus, like the fishermen who had fished for a living all their lives or the tax collectors who had only pursued money, must have had a hard time to learn to perceive Jesus as the Son of God, even though they may have heard in their minds, "He is the Son of God sent to the world" or "He is the One we are waiting for."

Now if we compare what a fisherman or a farmer is concentrated on everyday to what a priest or a cleric is focused on doing, it is surely different. If we observe the life of these religious leaders, we can say that they are mainly focusing on seeing specific objects as holy in the process of performing the temple rituals. So if we heard that Jesus went to see those priests first before turning to the world of manual laborers, we can understand why he would do so. Jesus knew that the priests and the rabbis had many long years of training to view physical objects as more than just matter; therefore based on their background, Jesus knew they were capable of believing he came as the holy Son of God, especially if God revealed to them this prophetic word.

In other words, Jesus knew that if he performed some kind of miracle in the presence of these clergy, they would not just see him as a miracle maker, but in that moment they would receive a message from God about him, which would be the real miracle. Maybe some of them did hear, "This is the Lamb of God, who takes away the sin of the world" (John 1:29), or some words connected to this idea. For this reason, if we look at Jesus' life and what he wanted people to believe in relation to who he was, it is natural that he would go to the religious people first because they had been trained to make the vertical line for many years.

When Jesus found himself obliged to go to the fishermen and other kinds of people whom we consider are more materialistic or centered on the horizontal line, Jesus must have known he would not be the Lord of glory but the Lord of suffering. This was because this group of disciples was not his first choice, because he had to train them to believe in the vertical line in connection to material objects.

When we see this situation of Jesus having to leave the people who were trained to believe in the vertical line, this can help us imagine the difficulties Jesus must have faced in finding people who could start to believe in the word of God in the midst of their secular life, regardless maybe some of them received a revelation when they came in contact with Jesus. But because these men and women he had to turn to did not have any training in maintaining a divine thought toward matter, they had difficulty to maintain faith or believe in the words connecting Jesus to God, regardless these words could have come from God Himself. Surely after making effort so many times, near the end of his life Jesus must have concluded that all he could do was to give them some simple physical objects to help them, and eventually all humankind, to connect to his holiness. Therefore as a remembrance, he took the occasion at the Passover meal to tell his disciples, "This is my body given for you; do this in remembrance of me" (Luke 22:19).

If today we have the time, patience, and perseverance to practice this view that Jesus has left with us, we too will find the vertical axis and we will be able to feel his love coming to us when we participate in the ceremony of the bread and the wine, or perhaps through other moments as well. And through this experience it should not be so difficult to carry the same concept wherever we go, that the flowers, the trees, and the multitude of other aspects of the creation are created as symbols of God's beauty and Christ's love. But until we have the instinct to take this viewpoint when we see something or when someone gives something to us, God cannot pour out His love to us. As well, we will not be able to give love back to Him, regardless we would like to respond to Him.

However, if we are able to put ourselves in the proper alignment, we will have discovered the most invisible law existing on this planet, which I call 'the law of love'. Every time we follow that law of love, we will be able to build our relationship with the One who is the source of that love.

This event of each one of us finding the law of love resembles another moment in history when someone discovered the law of gravity, which in its invisible aspect resembles the vertical line of the universe. Before this discovery, people didn't know why objects behaved the way they did; movements seemed like something magical. The moment human beings discovered the law of gravity, they quickly learned how to use that law. Among other things, humans became capable of flying because they understood the law that brings objects up and down.

Difference in Symbols

Now, if we start to practice carrying some thought or belief in connection to specific objects in order to receive God's love, we will realize that not every object allows us to receive the same amount of energy, even though we are in the perfect alignment with the law of love. For example, if we worship an animal like a cow, bearing in mind that it is a symbol of God, the triangle formed between us and the object of our worship plus God will allow us to receive a certain amount of feeling. Based on the law of the gravity of love, God will be obliged to give His love at least in some degree, because the moment of worshipping the animal is a moment of making ourself in some kind of alignment with God.

However, when we believe that human beings are created in the image of God, and we relate with each individual with that thought in mind, we will discover that we are able to receive a greater amount of feeling in comparison to when we carry that same view toward an animal. Through this experience we can realize that the quantity of love we are able to receive from God depends not only on our vertical axis, but on what object we choose as well. We can choose a mineral, like gold or silver, or a plant or an animal as a representative of God, but surely if we choose a human being as an expression of God's love, this alignment will make us perceive very different feelings.

Therefore, although minerals, plants, animals, and human beings were all initiated by God and are symbols of Him, their level of value is different. This means that not all symbols allow God to give to us the same amount of love, regardless we can perfect the thought that everything is a symbol of God. This is because, depending on how they are made, their capacities vary, and these variations create a hierarchy. If we worship a crystal or a metal, which stands at the beginning stage of the creation of God, we will receive a certain amount of energy, but it will be less than if we worship an animal like a goat or a lamb, and much less than if we view human beings as symbols or images of God.

This is the reason throughout history human beings have chosen different objects like a mountain, or the sun, moon and stars, or an animal to learn to create this vertical line through worshipping them. And if humans made a change in the object of their worship, it is because they discovered that the quantity of feeling they experienced when they worshipped the new object was higher.

The reason humans change the object of faith, called changing religions, is because human beings are constantly looking for more energy to maintain their existence. For example, modern humans demand more energy to keep their cities bright for twenty-four hours, so they can have more hours in the day to do things. This is not only so we can be more productive, but more importantly, it is for the purpose of making more duality each day, so our hearts can be filled up with love. Basically, human beings are always looking for the next entity that will permit us to receive higher energy.

How much energy or love humans experience with particular aspects of the creation will determine how much time they will want to spend with each object. Based on this reality, we do not see human beings wanting to marry an ant, a hamster or a dog, even though they often accept to have a dog as a companion for the length of the dog's life. We see humans basically wanting to be married to another human being. We can say this is primarily because humans feel a greater quantity of love through relating with another human being than they can feel with other objects.

Due to our desire to find greater energy, there will always be some person who will try to find a new symbol that will permit him or her to receive the greatest love. This is the reason some religious thinkers realized that if they chose a special human being, one who is not corrupted but who is sanctified, they can use this person as a symbol of God in order to receive more love.

The Realm of God's Words

There is another category of worship, which comes in-between the level of worshipping an inanimate object or an animal and worshipping a holy human being. This category entails believing in certain words as the symbols of God. This is the reason we see many individuals who have the tendency to read words intensely. This affinity for words is not merely for the sake of information, but it is because these people have discovered a secret source of energy, which comes out from the words from time to time.

Religious people have discovered that every time they read the words they believe must have come from God, like for example the Bible, the Torah or the Koran, they experience an energy which brings them to a higher dimension. For this reason, if you have ever experienced dialoguing with people who believe the words they read were inspired by God, and if you happen to express different or new views to them, they many times appear to be threatened by your views. And the reason for this agitation is because you are not just engaging in an intellectual discussion with them, you are also touching the emotions they have received in connection to their holy books. Because of the feelings they have experienced, religious people can have difficulty abandoning or changing their beliefs, regardless the person who comes to them is coming to present a greater thought so they can experience a greater feeling. Due to their convictions, they will even give up their lives to uphold the words of their books.

On another level, religious people fight hard not to change their beliefs because they do not want to lose the energy they have received from God, since it is all they have. And regardless they may not fully understand the contents of what they are reading, connecting those words to God permits them to receive some quantity of energy, giving them added value as individuals. Therefore, if someone approaches them with new words, often they will feel threatened, as if the new words will cause them to lose the energy they have been receiving, based on their knowledge, for years. They feel that if something can affect their belief, they will lose the value they have gained.

Due to this complex event, we can understand why religious people can fall in love with the words that they read and believe so strongly in them. And if it is true that the love of God can come through the process of believing, then we can also question, is it possible that we can receive greater or lesser amounts of energy or love based on which words we believe in? If people believe in words that are not one hundred percent equal to God's idea, will the love that God wants to give to them be the same as for those who believe in words that are one hundred percent of what God wants to say?

Surely to find this answer, we can look at relationships between human beings. If one human being does not understand another human being's viewpoint, will the feeling be the same as between two human beings who hold the same view? As we know, when we misunderstand each other, our feelings are very different than when we understand each other.

Based on this everyday reality, let's suppose that the words we are reading, which were written many years ago, are not exactly one hundred percent what God wanted to say, but rather reveal fifty percent of what God wanted to say. Regardless we may believe these words come from God, can we consider the love we can receive from words that are barely fifty percent truthful can be equal to the love we can receive through words that are maybe seventy-five percent true? And if one day we find the absolute truth of God, will the love we can receive be greater than when we believed in something that was only partially true or maybe even false?

New Words, Deeper Love

Regardless some religious groups have maintained their beliefs in words that were written hundreds or thousands of years ago, if a new group suddenly appears and presents a new understanding of what God wants to say about the meaning of our lives, these elder religious groups might be surprised to realize that if they can open their minds to accept and believe this new understanding, they can receive a greater amount of love from God than they were receiving through their ancient words. If some start to receive more energy or more love from a new explanation, people will surely be attracted to this new belief and little by little will begin to move away from their former beliefs. If people could have the freedom to choose the words they want to believe without being persecuted, it would be natural to see many people shifting their beliefs during their lives, eventually changing from one denomination to another, and even to another religion. Considering the connection between thought and feelings, it would be considered a natural process to change religions, since we all want to understand better what God wants to say to us, and to experience God deeper within us as we grow and mature through the process of our lives.

If a person has discovered some understanding that he dearly believes symbolizes the presence of God or someone holy, the words he will proclaim over and over are, "These words are true." The reason he can make this statement is because he receives some energy when he hears or reads those words, which manifests in a sense of confidence. Also, because that person experienced some feelings from certain words, he will have the tendency to categorize all the other words he reads from his book as 'true', and due to this may close himself to any words outside of his book.

Because many believers claim they have the one and only truth, this shows us that those who are the defenders of their beliefs must have, to some degree, received a certain quantity of energy when they were reading and believing in their texts. Based on this connection or closeness of understanding that brings more love, if we find someone who has a lot of energy or love already within himself, it means this person must have discovered and believed in words that were closer to God's idea, and these words allowed him to receive a greater quantity of emotion from God.

If we as humans are interested in having a stronger relationship with God, then we have to be sincere about how we distinguish one group of beliefs from another. For example, if we have been taught that God is a good Being who created us and if we accept to believe that this world is a good world symbolizing God's goodness, then surely some of His love will come to us. And if we also believe that God is our Father who has love toward us who stand in the position of His children, then surely the amount of love we will receive will be higher than the amount we could receive from the previous belief.

Not every word or thought has the same power regardless they all may have some connection to God. The words we choose to believe determine where we stand before God. Because not every word allows God's love to be released equally, the words that more closely describe the real condition of God will allow us to receive more love. This is the reason we can we see Jesus must have understood the law that physical matter plus a certain thought creates feelings, because according to the Bible he said that those who believe in him would go to the Kingdom of Heaven. But when Jesus said to his disciples at another time to drink the wine from the cup and eat of the bread, he did not say they would go to the Kingdom of Heaven.

Instead he said, "...do this in remembrance of me" (Luke 22:19).

If we look at this meal called the Last Supper, we can see there are many ways to view the events of that meal. The act of lifting his cup of wine could be seen as a banal gesture of offering a toast in celebration. Another person could say this act of Jesus lifting the cup of wine and the piece of bread is an act with historical value because it portrays the customs of that time. Still another person can view Jesus' action of lifting the cup and distributing the bread as symbols that will bring us eternal life if we believe in them.

If we observe these three views of the same event, we can find three completely different understandings coming from different angles. If we want to discover the real meaning, we can say that one view must be more vertical than the others and that this view, which is closer to the truth, will allow us to receive a higher degree of love than the more horizontal views. Surely, any person who believes that the bread and the cup of wine symbolize the body and blood of Christ will experience a greater amount of love when he or she partakes in that ceremony than a person who believes either of the other two views.

Because Jesus understood the value of the thought behind the physical object in order to be able to receive the love of God, he insisted that the people who believed in him should practice this ceremony. This is the reason he basically said, every time you drink this wine and eat this bread, you are not drinking and eating the physical ingredients only, you are receiving another ingredient, which is my love. Through this presentation, Jesus was hoping that the people would maintain their belief in these symbols and therefore be able to receive his love for a long period of history, until the next Son of God could come.

For this reason, those believers who have had the experience of receiving Jesus' love through this ceremony still wish to invite other people to their services, so that they can experience the same thing. However, if their guests do not have any concept of what the bread and wine symbolize, we should not be surprised to see them responding with indifference to that ceremony or questioning why the ones who invited them want to participate in such a ceremony.

In this situation, regardless how much you want the person to be interested in the events taking place, you realize that you will not be successful until you first explain the life of Jesus and the events of the Last Supper. If this person accepts to believe in your explanation, in that moment she will create the horizontal base in order to find the vertical axis, which will permit her to be able to feel what you feel if she partakes in that ceremony. If she can create these two lines, this person will eventually be capable of coming into communion with the One you are in communion with. If your friend is able to discover this secret, surely you will feel happy to know that someone close to you has discovered a higher dimension of love that was imperceptible to her before.

We can now realize that it is not just the object we focus on that is important, but the correct understanding around that object or symbol is necessary in order to capture the essence of that emotional realm. For example, if you accept the idea that God is the owner of all the creation, in that moment He can release some part of His heart to you. But if you cannot agree to accept God as the Creator and instead act as if the creation happened through a random process, then although the creation may appear impressive to you, you will not have much emotion toward it. If you cannot find the best viewpoint, then all the love God wants to transmit to you through the creation, or directly, cannot be given to you.

Therefore the way we think concerning the physical Earth and what is living around us determines how much we are able to experience the love of the Creator. Based on our whether or not we are able to receive love, our physical behavior will take a certain pattern, which is to care or not to care about others and the world around us. Based on this result, it is crucial for us to find the best thought for the miracle of love to take place.

If we consider the Earth came into existence by some random process, having no original Creator and no original design, we can only value ourselves as being nothing more than a gathering of molecules with the potential to reproduce another physical being. Due to the absence of an origin, we will be obliged to not have any feeling toward whom we live with or toward ourselves. Such a view prohibits us from being aware of God and therefore blocks the way for us to receive His love. The result of this lack of love can only be to stifle our feelings for each other, even to the point that we can destroy someone's life without even being confronted by our conscience.

If we look at the reactions of matter with the view that there is no invisible realm like physics, mathematics or chemistry behind what we see, we would have to believe that matter reacts through its own ingenuity or by coincidence. But if we believe there is an internal world of physics behind matter, it should not be difficult to also believe that behind our bodies' processes, there is a world of thought directing the way our characters are being formed.

Most human beings have accepted to go behind physical matter and discover the more invisible world of knowledge, however, this evolution has led us to an interesting scenario. Those who accept the spiritual realm may wonder: How is it possible that human beings, who have lived on this Earth for so long, can remove the concept that there is a Creator who originated the creation? On the other hand, more secularly oriented people might ask, "How can we possibly accept to look at physical objects and interpret them as symbols of God?"

If we are sincere with ourselves, we can wonder how one human species can look at the creation with two completely opposite views toward it. We can ask if it is because human beings come from two different origins that we can have such different views? Or is it simply because our brains are so highly pervaded with a view of opposition that we have the tendency to make different choices? One thing we can observe is that most people see life based on matter alone, and a smaller group will strive to add some thought to matter, connected to the invisible world of emotion and eventually God.

The focus people have and the choices they make will define them as being interested in either the visible dimension of this world or the invisible dimension. Based on their choices, either to become materialistic or spiritual, they will experience different amounts of feeling within themselves, and different kinds of emotions. Through their choices we can find some sweet characters and many sour ones.

The Physical Body as a Symbol of God

Even though the world has received some education concerning the use of a few objects as symbols of God or as symbols of the Christ, we can ask, how many physical symbols do we have the right to use in order to help us to discover the world of emotion? An even bigger question we can ask is, can we also consider our own physical bodies as being symbols of God?

If we evaluate our lives based on the possibility that our physical bodies are meant to be symbols of God, we will experience new emotions from God. And if we can maintain this view that our bodies are symbols of God for a long period of time, we will be able to experience the joy of God manifesting Himself in us. The greater the amount of joy we experience, the more it will become clear that this understanding is close to the original idea of why God created human beings, as we find in Colossians 3:10: "…(you) have put on a new self, which is being renewed in knowledge in the image of its Creator."

On the other hand, if we cannot accept or maintain the thought of our selves as symbols of God, then it is understandable why we would rather choose other objects as symbols, because this thought is easier to maintain. This is the reason many religions prefer to choose specific rituals or specific objects to represent the divinity of God instead of choosing their own physical bodies as symbols of God. Therefore, if someone comes and claims, "When you see me, you see the Father," these religious people will respond, "How can you say you are a symbol of God when we already have our rituals and symbols of God?"

Due to the difficulty of the people around Jesus to accept the view that he was the physical Son of the Father in Heaven, people began to reject him instead of humbling themselves and saying, "This young man must have achieved something really special in order to say these words." Because people began to persecute him, Jesus found himself having to introduce the idea that when they drank from the cup and ate the bread it was symbolically like drinking his blood and eating his flesh. But Jesus knew that by introducing these symbolic objects, he was establishing a new religion similar to the religion that he came from, where people believed that God existed within the Ark of the Covenant and the bread of atonement.

Regardless of the sad reality of the past, we should seriously ask ourselves the question, should we also only recognize the chalice of wine and the bread called the host that is given in our church services as symbols of the body and blood of Jesus? Or every time we drink from any cup could we think it symbolizes his blood? Should we be limited to only recognizing the bread that is given at the church service as being the symbol of the body of Our Lord, or every time we eat any bread or see rolls in a bakery can we remember that they symbolize the body of Jesus? From a theological aspect, would this view make us heretics or would it actually allow us to meet Jesus more often in our daily life?

Once we train ourselves to recognize all that is created by the Almighty God as symbols of God's heart, this thought will allow us to be qualified to become beings who can also carry that heart. The moment we start to experience the core of God's love, which has seemed to some people to be a mysterious or even fearful event and considered private and personal, we will realize that this vibration or emotion is exactly what we all dream to have, especially if we want to one day present ourselves as worthy of belonging to the Christ or to his God.

For example, if we can see not just the material aspect of a tree but also see the tree as a symbol of Christ, we can have an awareness of the tree's majesty and how it reflects the all-emcompassing love of Christ. The combination of thoughts we have about the tree will allow us to more fully admire both Christ and the tree. Due to this admiration, which combines vertical and horizontal viewpoints, we will be likely to plant trees next to our house for the purpose of providing shade and beauty and, as well, to serve as a constant reminder of the loving and protective nature of Christ.

Even if someone studies plant, animal and human biology with the view that everything is just matter, eventually he cannot help but be surprised about the things he discovers, to the point he might hear a question coming from deep within his mind asking, "How is it possible everything has so much complexity and sophistication? Doesn't this intricate design reflect someone great behind it?" However, if the student is determined to keep the view of materialism, he will reject the thought that this physical creation could be a symbol of an invisible Creator's heart or that the majestic physiology of the human body is actually an extension of the complexity of the Creator's imagination.

However, if the student is not afraid to feel a lot of emotion, then his laboratory is just the right place to eagerly look at the human body as the most majestic system imaginable. And if he humbles himself and takes the view that we human beings must have been engineered by someone much, much greater than ourselves, surely he or she will be discovering the perfect thought that will allow him to see humans in the same way as God may see them.

We can agree that no matter how much we study, the view we choose will ultimately determine what we are capable of feeling. We have to understand that our view toward what exists places us in a very specific position. For example, if we categorize whatever we study as being purely physical and existing without purpose or direction, this thought will surely not help us value what we study. By not connecting what we study to its value in relation to God, we will be unable to receive positive energy because this position shatters the connection with God.

It is the same as if we have a phone in our home and our friends have a phone but our phone service is not activated to let our voices pass over the airwaves. No matter how long we wait by the phone to receive some news, we will never be able to receive the connection. Comparatively, if human beings do not have any special thought when they see something or someone, they cannot receive any positive emotion toward the things and the people around them. And if they do not feel anything but still have to lead active lives, they will eventually feel more drained day by day, which we call emotional isolation.

On the other hand, if you consider that your physical body is not just a physical object but also a symbol representing God's heart, then God's love will be directed throughout your body. Through this experience you will realize that everything you see transmits eternal energy because when you connect what you see to God.

For example, suppose one day you decide to read the book known as the Bible. You may realize that this book is filled with many interesting stories, some appearing to be miraculous, and some appearing to be scandalous. As well, you can sense that this book offers some historical view of what might have happened in the past. You may even find yourself learning about the political system of that time period. However, a historical view alone will not allow you to understand the symbolism hidden behind each story. A historian will not consider the Bible as a book to promote faith and surely not as having the potential to give rebirth to human beings. Instead he will scrutinize it for hints about historical events, or look for any illogical concepts or contradictions in order to justify his disregard for it.

However, if another person reads the same book but has been trained to see the symbols of each event or story as being part of a mystical code of God, this person will be able to find enlightenment and therefore will find his inner self becoming quite calm and peaceful because he is finding what God wanted to say. Accepting that God initiated the stories in the Bible to some degree, even though many of them are not completely understandable, acceptable or even believable, has surely allowed millions of people to receive new inspiration and energy from God and caused them to behave differently. The effect of such an emotional experience can transform people's lives in a positive way, which is why so many consider the Bible has given them rebirth.

Origin of the Word

Why is it that people can view the Bible in so many different ways? Let us imagine reading a verse from the section of the Bible called the New Testament. Since we know that Jesus himself didn't write down his words and therefore the words that are attributed to him were maybe not actually spoken by Jesus himself, we could perhaps question the authenticity of those words. However, if we believe that Jesus was the only one who could possible say words such as, 'Those who are humble will be the ones to enter the Kingdom of Heaven' we would still consider them to be part of Jesus' viewpoint, and due to our thought that those words were connected to Jesus, we would feel positive vibrations coming to us through those words.

However, if we read those same words and begin analyzing them, questioning whether they were really spoken by Jesus or written by his disciples or some person decades later, we might start to say, "Because they were not written by Jesus himself I do not want to believe in them anymore." This thought will break the connection between us and the words that Jesus could have spoken and, as a result of our rejection, those words will no longer allow us to feel the vibration of love from God. Actually, this choice will make us feel empty.

After explaining these possibilities, we can see that the word alone does not have the power to make us feel the energy of God. It is only when we connect the word to its origin, and especially if we admire this origin, that we will be capable of receiving a lot of positive emotion. For example, if a person reads the New Testament with the viewpoint that the words were spoken by Jesus regardless that they were written by someone else, this reader will be capable of receiving more love than the one who reads those words without acknowledging Jesus who was said to have spoken those words.

What if we look at mathematics and believe that it is just pure knowledge? Now we know what will happen. We will get bored and begin to question why we have to learn math. But if we suddenly look at this knowledge as being a special language from the brain of God, then I think we will view mathematics with excitement and at the same time we will have more recognition of the genius of God.

Traditionally, we have always perceived the words in the Bible as belonging to God. And because there are so many people who want to have a connection to God, they have the tendency to want to read this book. But if we want to be fascinated by God and acknowledge His genius, I think we should also look closely at mathematics and science. Through our studies we will more easily believe that God is Almighty. But because religious people haven't chosen the book of Science or Mathematics to glorify God, those books haven't acquired their full value, and many times the knowledge in them is instead used to disgrace God and to deny Him.

The reason I use this example is to show how human beings have a tendency to connect some things to God and to disassociate other things from God. The choice human beings make in this process of thinking creates disunity within themselves by separating what is spiritual and what is physical, and as well creates disunity within their civilization.

Expanding our Symbols of Christ

Let us look at a time in the history of Western civilization called the Middle Ages, when human beings must have discovered a desire to create different symbols of God and they began to build the great cathedrals. Through their designs, the clergy were hoping the edifices they were constructing would represent more than just beautiful works of art to show off the talent of the builders. Regardless these buildings demanded so much money, the archbishops who initiated the cathedrals did not only value them as a place where all the rich of the city could gather on Sundays, but they were hoping that the people who gave donations or worked on the construction of the cathedral would connect thoughts of God and Jesus Christ to that edifice, in hope that these thoughts would help them to have a greater place in heaven.

Surely this viewpoint would allow the people to feel something good as they approached those buildings and gazed up at the majestic shapes and high steeples reaching up into the heavens. And when they entered those buildings and saw the stained glass windows and lofty arches, they could have felt illuminated and elevated.

Now, if we can take our viewpoint to a higher level, by looking at these same buildings with the view that they not only represent God or Jesus but also that we ourselves should be living temples who come to worship the first True Living Temple, surely this thought will allow us receive more emotion from God, because this thought is closer to the concept Jesus was trying to give to us when he said, "Destroy this temple, and I will raise it again in three days" (John 2:19). If everyone in the church or cathedral believes he or she is also the living temple of God who has come to worship the Christ, surely this will attract more people to come inside this building, to the point they will call themselves 'the house of God.' If people can carry this vertical thought in the midst of observing the lofty design of their place of worship, they will not just feel happy to go to church, but they will also begin to feel the presence of God personally coming close to them.

Yet today the view of seeing a cathedral as a house of God has started to fall away, replaced by other thoughts that look more secular. Due to these secular or horizontal thoughts, many people visit these buildings as if they were museums that simply contain interesting historical artifacts and architectural styles. Among the people going inside an ancient cathedral, we seldom see anyone approaching it as a place where they can pray or with the faith that maybe they would be healed by God, like the person in Jesus' time who touched his robe, believing she would be healed by doing so.

Indeed these buildings, which were originally constructed to symbolize the dwelling place of God and have been used as part of the process of saving people for a few hundred years, must feel sad in these days because they are not recognized as having the same value any more. If God also has been watching these events, He might be concerned and wondering, "…If human beings do not see physical objects as symbols, how can they learn to create the vertical line? …How can they possible perceive My heart for them when I bring the One who resembles Me?"

On the other hand, maybe God is observing human beings with the hope that they can find other symbols even better than these cathedrals, by recognizing the many symbols which already exist around their daily lives. Maybe God wishes that we would trip and fall head-first into a bed of pansies and by bumping our noses into the blossoms we would recognize His love and beauty within them. Or maybe He hopes that when our skin gets scratched by the thorn of a rosebush and we shed a drop of blood, we can still think of this event as symbolic of the One who is invisible, knowing that if we can look with a vertical viewpoint we can begin the process to receive one drop of God's love.

Indeed God knows that we humans will discover, as we continue our journey, that the depth of our thoughts connecting Him with the physical objects around us will determine the amount of energy we are able to receive. Therefore He will not be worried if we do not look at the cathedral as the most holy edifice because He will see people turning their thoughts toward Him with a multitude of objects around their lives. And if this is what is happening, we can know that the ranges of emotions human beings can experience will be remarkably varied and exciting.

For this reason, once we discover the thoughts that are closest to the intention of the One who originated the physical creation, this knowledge will have a higher value than all the knowledge concerning the names and structures of the creation around us. In other words, when we have the symbolic divine knowledge of why the cathedral, for example, was created, this will grant us permission to open our senses in order to experience the energy that resides inside that building. Or, when we walk in a garden and see the beautiful flowers, plants and trees as symbols of the invisible God, we surely will begin to feel energy coming from that creation, and eventually we can even have the sense that we are one with that energy and ultimately one with God.

So if you have the experience of going inside a cathedral, temple or mosque with an analytical viewpoint, which means that you will see only see the matter, you will perceive that building as similar to any other piece of grand architecture. Due to this viewpoint, you will not perceive it as the house of God and as a divine place, but you will classify it as a meeting hall or a space available for many different kinds of activities. Instead of considering this building as a place where you can develop a relationship with God, it will become a place where you can experience deep loneliness due to the horizontal line you have created toward it.

From this example, we can see why human beings react differently toward the same object, which in this case is a cathedral. The difference in their reactions is not because they carry different genes but because they choose different thoughts toward that object. So if tomorrow human beings choose to look at the flowers in their garden as divine symbols, surely their experience will be different than if they look at those flowers just to memorize their Latin names or to study them like specimens.

Therefore, we can define a real believer in God's viewpoint as someone who considers the building where he lives, the place where he works, and the environment around him as representations of God. On the other hand, the nonbeliever or partial believer is someone who analyzes what he sees without any thought in relation to what the invisible God would like for him to see.

According to this new definition, it is difficult to say that there are any real or true believers. Instead, there are plenty of people who read, plenty of people who speak, and plenty of people who try to have some beliefs. But there are not so many people who have been able to achieve the belief that every object they see is a symbol of the invisible God, maybe because it requires of them to have a strong vertical focus in order to maintain the awareness of everything as a symbol of God. However, if we want to achieve what Jesus became before he could start his appearance to the public, we as humans have to take this path and exercise this vertical focus with the same intensity that people usually exercise their horizontal mind to obtain knowledge through memorization and analysis.

Although human beings have already discovered many amazing secrets about the physical world, they have discovered very little about God. Because we focus on the horizontal mind, which is easy to do, we have a tendency to neglect the vertical line. But regardless of the difficulty, it is necessary for us humans to develop this vertical line in order to value ourselves. At the same time, the vertical line is also necessary to help us taste the flavor of God's love, to hear God's voice, and to smell the fragrance of God, not just through our spiritual senses but through the physical things we taste, hear, and smell.

If we humans can learn to connect physical things to different aspects of God, then we will become intoxicated with God's love. But since the vertical view of physical objects, in other words the divine aspect of physical objects, has not been emphasized by religion nor become a priority in our educational system, no one has considered this viewpoint to be important. Regardless the core of Jesus' teaching emphasizes this vertical line, it is often brushed aside, perhaps because it is not mandatory for our daily survival and doesn't look like it will give us a better salary.

Indeed, most people, including religious leaders, have forgotten this center of life. But if we wish to achieve harmonious relationships with each other as well as to create a society where we value people and things, we need to find the ingredient called love, which comes through the vertical line.

So surely, if what we want is not the dream but the reality of love, then we will need to reconsider this vertical viewpoint and give it a value that is at least equal to a horizontal, pragmatic view. Finding this vertical viewpoint is necessary not only to improve the quality of our physical lives but also for the enhancement of our eternal lives, whose existence many of us have not even considered.

Throughout history, human beings have discovered that if we have knowledge about what exists around us, that knowledge will help us to communicate with other human beings who have the same knowledge. If someone does not have the privilege of gaining knowledge about the physical things around him, this person will be condemned to be at the bottom of the hierarchy of knowledge. Seeing this as a major cause for the social gap within our world, many educators have felt their mission is to distribute secular knowledge to everyone, with the hope that their efforts to bridge the gap of knowledge could create an end to the hierarchy of social classes.

But now we know that the cause of this social gap between human beings comes from the different qualities of character that people carry within themselves. Therefore, to bridge this gap, people need to elevate their characters by focusing on the vertical viewpoint, which gives them the opportunity to relate equally with each other and to have the ability to receive the same quantity of God's love.

From Two-dimensional to Three-dimensional Beings

Christians have promoted the thought that Jesus is the greatest man on Earth who came to save the ones who believe in him, and through this thought, many people have changed the direction of their lives. Based on his ability to change people's lives, we can say that Jesus came as the substantial image of God's love. Therefore, if we accept to be educated to look at Jesus as being one of the first physical human beings who could achieve the standard of being the living incarnation of God's love, surely this thought will satisfy God, because it is close to the reality of how God views Jesus. As well, this viewpoint will allow us to discover that we also have the chance to become incarnations of God's love, instead of believing we have to isolate ourselves from this dream.

For this reason we can say that this thought towards Jesus can affect the destiny of our lives, if we choose this knowledge and use it daily. If humans decide to make this effort, the transformation will direct them to become higher quality people.

For example, if we consider Jesus was born of God and that we cannot achieve what he achieved because we are sinners, this thought will only allow us to receive a small amount of love from God, because we will believe that we as sinners can have nothing to do with Christ. More drastically, this thought can direct us to choose to be more passive or lenient with ourselves because we think we can do nothing to change our destiny.

And if our religious education is based on the memorization of verses, as if we needed to pass a test every seven days, we will only be able to perceive God's word with an intellectual viewpoint. This viewpoint can only allow us to be two-dimensional, or 'flat' beings, and because of that it will be impossible for us to be qualified to receive

God's love, regardless of our desire to be filled up with the love of God.

However, there is another shape we should also introduce. This is a spherical shape, which is composed of three dimensions. We know from our physical bodies that we are not made flat like sheets of paper, but rather have within ourselves organs like our livers, hearts, and brains. But regardless of how our physical bodies may appear, we still hear comments from people that they feel so flat or empty. What is interesting is when people say this phrase, we have the tendency to believe it is not referring to their physical form or to their stomachs being empty, but we have the sense they are referring to something within themselves that feels empty, which we call their souls.

From this, we can see that human beings are made to be three-dimensional, and the reason is because a human carries within himself a soul with the capacity to receive God's love. The nature of this soul is such that when it is empty, a human being feels 'hunger pangs' or the pain of emptiness. Therefore, in order to relieve these 'hunger pangs', we need to find the way to receive God's love.

If we only read our religious books as just a source of knowledge to memorize, then we can only remain as two-dimensional beings. But if we can read our books in order to learn something for our own lives, we will begin to perceive that the lives of people like Noah, Moses and Abraham do not just provide us with good stories, but we can see that these people were trying to do something to have a relationship with God.

If we take the three-dimensional viewpoint and perceive the people involved in those stories from the Bible or the Torah as actual people just like ourselves, then surely we will feel that this book is a book of life, because it helps us to receive the love of God. The love we feel will be similar to the love God had for those people when they were alive on Earth and striving to fulfill His will. As a result of these feelings coming to us, we will be able to understand some of the deeper messages which the stories have been keeping for us, which will allow us to direct our own lives with greater wisdom.

The moment we begin to perceive that the Bible is about real people who lived real lives, we will gain some feeling for them, and then we will be able to testify that the Bible is filled with stories of people who wanted to do God's will, which is to give life. After gaining this perception, we will recognize that the stories also portray the trail of the invisible God's heart toward those central people who were trying to do His will. Therefore, from this new perspective, instead of seeing these people who lived from 2,000 to 6,000 years ago as imaginary people, we will be able to identify ourselves with those people as being our brothers and sisters, as our fathers and mothers and even as our king. The reason we can perceive them this way is because we experience God's love for them in the midst of reading and studying about their lives, regardless the events took place so very long ago.

If we can look at the personage of Jesus with the three-dimensional view, we will not consider his life as just a nice story about a simple man who came in the midst of a people at a certain time in history. We will realize that Jesus was a real physical human being like each one of us and that whatever he said was not just something to believe but something for human beings to drive their lives by. Based on this three-dimensional view, we will realize that whatever history may or may not have recorded about the life of Jesus, his story is not fictitious but it demonstrates that Jesus really was alive and that he came to achieve what God asked him to do.

Once we realize that Jesus was a three-dimensional person in whom God's love could dwell, surely our feelings toward him will change, and our hearts will pulsate and melt and will deeply desire to go to him. With this view toward Jesus, we will be able to receive all the love that God has for him. Due to this experience of receiving God's love for Jesus, we will consider that we have discovered for the first time our very own private relationship with Jesus, which for so long has been unattainable because we have been educated to see all that is around us as matter instead of as symbols of God's heart. Therefore, if God so loved Jesus and if we have the right three-dimensional viewpoint, we will be able to feel the love of God passing through us to Jesus. But until we find this three-dimensional view, we should not be surprised to find ourselves indifferent to God or to Jesus and others in the Bible who tried to fulfill God's will.

Surely God as a Parent must know that it is not pleasant for people to only have one or two specific, ceremonial objects to use in remembrance of Him, especially if they worship often throughout their life, the same as their predecessors did for many centuries. The Israelites for a long period of time were looking at an object like the Ark of the Covenant and keeping the belief that this object symbolized God's power, however God was hoping that the religious people who practiced this vertical thought toward the object of faith would be capable of receiving His masterpiece when God presented a pure human being to them.

God Sends His Beloved Son

The reason God prepares so many religious people, still today, is to educate them to discover the secret of aligning themselves with the vertical line in order to begin to receive God's love. At the same time God is hoping those religious people will be able to reach the perfect 'zero' point where they will be humble enough to be prepared to meet the Son of God when he is presented to them.

Indeed, God will want to present His Son to them because He knows that even if religious people devote their lives to being faithful to an object of faith, these people will still be receiving less love than in the day when they can be in front of the one person who has achieved the perfect image of God as a human being. This is why, in Jesus' time, God was hoping the religious people would transfer their reverence for their objects of faith to the person God called His Masterpiece, especially since those people were waiting to welcome the One who was to come for so many hundreds of years.

Surely if the clergy of that time long ago could have accepted the words they received from Heaven when they came into the presence of this personage, it would have meant they were aligning themselves well with the vertical line. And even though they may have heard in their inner mind some prophesy about the person whom God called 'His Son', the question is, did they welcome that person or not? If they really had recognized Jesus, God would have injected all of His love for His Son into those religious people. And if they could have changed the focus of their worship from the Ark to the human person Jesus, this new focus would have allowed them to receive the love of God, which eventually would have made them one with Him.

Based on this historical situation, if we are concerned about being able to recognize that special person who is the living image of God, it will be favorable for us to learn the theory and philosophy that teaches us to see everything as symbols of God's love. If all the schools of thought would teach this idea of finding the perfect vertical alignment with God from a young age, all people would be able to receive enough love to sustain them until the time they could meet the Son of God.

Then when they could welcome this Beloved One, they would receive God's love directly. And by maintaining this thought for the rest of their lives, they would continuously receive God's abundant love every day, which would become visible in their flesh, to the point they would achieve the same result as Jesus did. As it is written, Jesus said, "Don't you believe that I am in the Father, and that the Father is in me? The words I say to you are not just my own. Rather, it is the Father, living in me, who is doing his work" (John 14:10).

I hope by now that you are beginning to understand that if you do not have this awareness to see everything as a symbol of God's love, then His love cannot reach you or flow through you. As we recall, there were some people who had the miraculous opportunity to be next to Jesus during his lifetime. But regardless they were next to him with their bodies, it looks like with their minds they could not perceive Jesus as the substantial living image of the invisible God. Because they could create the horizontal line, to some degree they could enjoy to be next to him due the atmosphere of love that he created; however, because they could not create the vertical line, very few of those people could maintain the divine thought that Jesus was the beloved Son of God. Perhaps they had many other thoughts that are not recorded in the Bible, especially during the time when turmoil and scandal surrounded Jesus, and due to this negativity, they surely could not maintain faith in him at that time as the Son of God. Due to this reality, it is understandable why later on they dismissed him as just a simple rabbi or whatever rumor had spread throughout Israel at that time.

Since the people did not value the vertical thought that God gave to them when they were next to Jesus, they could not find Jesus' depth or true nature, and as a result they were unable to experience the love God had for him. Instead of sharing God's viewpoint they saw him just like one of them, or as a human being who had many great talents, could do healings and could speak wisely, but not as God's Beloved Son.

Perhaps now we can read Jesus' story with the vertical thought that he was the living image of God's love, in addition to the fact that he was a physical being. With this vertical and horizontal line, we will be surprised to feel the love of God passing through us for him, two thousand years later. And because of this, we will find ourselves wanting to read his story carefully, a little at a time, because we do not want to miss any part of Jesus' life. The more we maintain the vertical and horizontal view about the events of Jesus' life as we are reading, the more our hearts will cry out for him and we will surely conclude, "Truly, you are the Son of God."

This conclusion will look similar to what happened to the disciples who were in the boat with Jesus during the storm and asked, "Who is this? He commands even the winds and the water, and they obey him" (Luke 8:25). And if you place yourself at the foot of Jesus' cross in the moment when the sky became dark and the earthquake shook the land, you will understand the centurion who was guarding Jesus when he exclaimed, "Surely this man was the Son of God" (Mark 15:39).

After all the events of Jesus' life and death had taken place, some people finally accepted to have the vertical thought that permitted them to recognize Jesus as the Son of God. This is the reason people began to receive revelations after Jesus' death and to cry out, "Oh my God, what have we done?" In Luke 23:48, it says that all the people who had gathered to witness the event of the cross beat their breasts after Jesus' death and went away from that place. Surely through this verse we can know that the people suddenly were given a glimpse that Jesus was a man in the direct image of God.

But due to the internal difficulties to find and to keep this vertical line, many people still today have difficulty to perceive Jesus as someone who carried the substance of God's love and continue to view him with a two-dimensional viewpoint formed by intellect alone. Due to this horizontal viewpoint, we see Jesus' life being spent in speaking many parables, like a storyteller, instead of someone who could give us life. Seeing Jesus this way limits the amount of feeling we can have for him, regardless God must have an immense amount of feeling for Jesus in order to dare to say, "You are my Son, whom I love; with you I am well pleased" (Luke 3:22).

If we can see Jesus as a divine human being, the one who represents the road that leads us to the love of God, we will be able to discover his whole life from the moment of his birth, through his teenage years and into his adulthood, and finally when his life ended. We will realize that he was truly an extraordinary human being, and when God sees us coming to that level of awareness, He will not wait an extra moment to flood our hearts with His love to show how much He still loves Jesus.

From this viewpoint, when someone presents a symbol like a cup of wine or a loaf of bread as representing the

Christ, we now understand how we can receive so much love by referring those objects to Jesus. After we experience this love toward Jesus, we will surely also discover the desire to find this vertical thought toward everything that was created, knowing how much Jesus cared about and referred to the natural world in his speeches. This way we will be able to experience the love of Christ throughout our lives, and if we can have this love with us, we will not be afraid if God calls us to expand our religious objects that are so precious to us, because we will know that as we enlarge our viewpoint of divinity, we will expand our experience of the love of God to a greater stage.

If we can educate ourselves to see everything around us as symbols of the character and nature of God, such as seeing someone doing a good deed and seeing the Christ in that person, we will discover the full nature of God's love. As we rise above our intellectual perceptions of life, we will re-value everything around our lives, especially other people like our parents, our families, our friends and all those around us. If we can begin to see our parents as symbols of God's love, we will discover ourselves feeling differently toward them than if we just consider them to be nice people who protected us when we were small children, and although we may live separately from them as we get older, we will find that we are still able to look at them as symbols of God's love.

On the other hand, if we cannot rise above the two-dimensional way of seeing all things, we can be sure that our children will look at us in the same way. They will see us only with an intellectual viewpoint and this will limit the amount of love they can feel for us. Perhaps our children will recognize what we did physically for them but nothing more will remain in them than a few souvenirs of different events. Without love in their souls, our children's attachment toward us will weaken as the years pass, until one day we will notice that their thoughts toward us are exactly the same as what we felt toward our own parents. They will see us as people who helped them to survive. Indeed this reality of heart will not change from generation to generation unless someone decides to create a strong vertical line above the horizontal line. If there is someone who does so, this one will lead us to create a new cycle of life, a spherical dimension.

By accepting to look at life with the viewpoint that everything is a symbol of God's love, we will no longer exist purely as biological beings. In other words, we will not be beings of chemical reactions and biological processes alone but we will become people of love, whom others will dearly respect. And by approaching life with this vertical thought, we will begin to discover why God created this majestic physical world around us before introducing human beings into its midst.

Surely we can say God must not have created the physical world for His own interest because He already had everything He needed to exist. But even though God had everything, there was one thing that God was missing, which was to have a partner to share His love with. Therefore, as a part of the process to help humanity to grow their love, God created the physical world and everything within it with the hope that human beings would learn to see Him through every object, until they were mature enough to relate with Him directly.

When humanity can achieve this level of maturity, we can say it is like an eighth day of creation, because we will have everything, including God, as our partner of love. Now it is clear that in order for human beings to become God's children, we have to receive His love first, and in order to do so we need first to learn to see all characteristics as being symbols of God's love.

If this lesson is new to us today, it means that it took 6,000 years or perhaps ten times 6,000 years for humans to discover the original purpose of why God created the physical world. Either way, I think it has been much too long for God to wait even one more day for us to discover the vertical line. Surely God will feel so hopeful if He can see us recognizing His creation as an extension of His love, because He knows that through this channel we will be able to nourish our eternal souls.

Since Jesus maintained this consciousness throughout his entire life, his heart and soul became the recipient of God's love, which formed his divine character and made him unique among humanity even until today. Regardless the people around Jesus may have had difficulty to perceive his divinity, like Mary, Martha and many others who lived around him in a very close way, Jesus maintained his dignity before his Father. And due to the fact that he did not lose his vertical line, regardless so many people tried to destroy it, he could not lose the love from God that he had received even when he was going to his own death.

Incredibly, each of us as human beings should follow the same destiny of character as Jesus, because Jesus was human just as we are, yet he found the way to be divine at the same time. Due to our having the same potential destiny as Jesus, we can accept his call, "Be perfect, therefore, as your heavenly Father is perfect" (Matt. 5:48). Jesus did not say these words for the sake of judging the people of his day or of today, if in case we still feel judged. He said these words because he believed that all human beings were created with the same purpose he had, which is to communicate with God and to become one with God on Earth first, before we can be sent to Heaven. To make us aware of what we should do, he said, "I tell you the truth, whatever you bind on Earth will be bound in Heaven, and whatever you loose on Earth will be loosed in Heaven" (Matt. 18:18).

Through this verse, which reflects his concern to see humans become one with God, we can begin to understand why Jesus addressed certain people concerning the rituals they performed in the temples. The reason he approached these priest was because Jesus wanted them to recognize that the purpose behind all of their rituals was for them to learn to align themselves vertically before God. But ultimately, the main purpose for this training, if not the only reason it was valuable, was to help those people recognize the One who had come to demonstrate the full potential of the human capacity to substantiate God's love. This is the reason Jesus said to them, "You diligently study the Scriptures because you think that by them you possess eternal life. These are the Scriptures that testify about me, yet you refuse to come to me to have life" (John 5:39-40).

Because of the lack of vertical thought by these historical people, we today still have to learn to use a divine thought in connection to all things. We need to look around us and learn to see things as symbols of God's love that we have never taken seriously, like trees, for example. Maybe the reason we never took trees as holy symbols is because they are too big to fit inside our temples and churches. But if we refer to the Bible, we can discover that the true man was symbolized by a tree, as it says in Rev. 22:14, "Blessed are those who wash their robes, that they may have the right to the tree of life and may go through the gates into the city."

As well as the botanical world, we can find in the Bible another symbol that we often walk upon—rocks. In Psalms 18:2, it is written, "The Lord is my rock, my fortress and my deliverer; my God is my rock, in whom I take refuge. He is my shield and the horn of my salvation, my stronghold." And in Rev. 2:17 we are told, "To him who overcomes, I will give ... a white stone with a new name written on it, known only to him who receives it."

Religions have not taken objects like the tree or the rock as symbols of their God in addition to their traditional ritualistic objects. But as we can see, the value of these items can be just as great as the cup, the unleavened bread, the ark or the lamp, to name a few.

Therefore, if we want to prepare ourselves to enter a greater dimension with this new understanding, we will start our days by saying, "Good morning" to others with the thought that they are symbols of the love of God. If this becomes our ritual every morning, this way of life will surpass any religious ritual performed in the past or in the present. If Jesus or Moses and Muhammad can see us discovering this view, surely they will be happy to see us performing such an internal tradition, because they know that we are beginning the road to fulfill the true meaning of human life on this Earth, as they achieved.

Now, if we feel that we are chosen, for whatever reason, to believe in the tradition of the love of God, this means that first of all we need to educate our minds to perceive everything as symbols of God's love. And if we are serious about this calling, then when we create a meal, we will use the viewpoint that all the ingredients in the meal are symbols of God's love, and our recognition of these symbols will allow God to give His love to those who receive the meals. Likewise, when we go to work every day to provide for our families with the view that we are working to show God's love, when we return home our families will see us as expressions of God's love, and as a family all of us will experience the love of God.

This is why Jesus said that when we do something for the least of our brothers or sisters, we do it for him. In Matt. 25:34-40 it is written, "Come, you who are blessed by my Father; take your inheritance, the kingdom prepared for you since the creation of the world. For I was hungry and you gave me something to eat, I was thirsty and you gave me something to drink, I was a stranger and you invited me in, I needed clothes and you clothed me, I was sick and you looked after me, I was in prison and you came to visit me."

Surely if we live with this awareness every moment of our days, after some time we will see ourselves changing because we will be able to receive love, that mysterious invisible nourishment for our souls. And through making this daily effort, we will discover that the most beautiful thing on Earth is to know that the purpose of our physical bodies is to grow our souls until they can contain all of the love of God. And although we may be happy to taste this love during our physical lifetimes, I believe we also hope that when we pass away we will be able to take all of this love with us wherever we go. If we understand this point then we will realize how serious our time on Earth is in connection to the length of eternity.

If we remind ourselves about the explanation of the cup of wine and the loaf of bread that our priest or minister offers to us as symbols of Jesus, we will realize that this is just the first-grade level of taking God's viewpoint. This ritual is just the beginning of making a proper vertical alignment in order to receive God's love. It is important to understand that it is not the cup of wine or the bread that saves us. Instead it is the love that God can give to us when we make the correct vertical alignment that transforms us, which means that having the highest thought in connection to those specific objects is actually very necessary, and this is what will make us feel that those objects are holy. Since the experience of God's love can make us feel healed from the sin that we carry, the feeling of rebirth can take place, which is also referred to as being resurrected.

If we recall a certain story from the Bible, a crowd was walking with Jesus when for some reason someone touched the hem of his robe. Jesus asked who touched him, and the disciples responded by saying that everyone there had touched him. But Jesus said that only one person had really touched him.

What was so special about this report is that in order for Jesus to notice there was someone who touched him, we can understand that this woman who approached Jesus must have looked at him with the viewpoint that he was the divine expression of God's love. Due to her viewpoint, God could transmit His love to her through Jesus when she touched his clothing. Regardless of the majesty of this single event, we can also say that his life story was a most tragic one, due to the fact that only this one person touched him with the three-dimensional viewpoint of admiration and glorification.

In the same way, if we touch our partner with the viewpoint that he or she is an expression of God's love, God will be able to allow His love to flow through us to our partner, and through this we will both be able to experience love. When human beings learn to have this three-dimensional viewpoint then surely this planet will be able to be described as a Garden of Eden.

Unless human beings can learn to live with a vertical viewpoint, they will stay dry, like a barren wilderness, thirsty, desperate and feeling no value, to the point of having no fear to destroy themselves or others. If we could hear the cry of humanity carrying the burden of not receiving God's love for so long, we would definitely declare that humanity is in a state of emergency. It is imperative therefore for human beings who have lived in this wilderness for so many years to learn the viewpoint that will permit them to receive God's love wherever they live.

Until we as adults pursue our destiny to be emotional people filled with love, we cannot become the children of God or inherit His kingdom of love. It was God's hope that we would live in this kingdom, a place that He prepared over a period of six very long 'days'. Upon the seventh day, God decided to visit His creation in order to make sure that everything had been made well, regardless of the complexities of the process. His standard of excellence was to bring His creation to the point where human beings could arrive to this garden and be able live there for eternity in love with Him as His children.

If we want to become God's children living in the Garden of Eden with our Heavenly Father and Mother, it is now understandable that the most perfect viewpoint we can have is the one that will allow us to become the same as our Parents. If we can begin to see that God created everything in the perfect image of His own Parental character and heart, then God Himself will assure us that we will not live with remorse for eternity but with happiness. This is the reason that on the seventh day of creation God was waiting to see if human beings could move from the position of children to the position of parents, which is the real image of God. Unfortunately, God realized that no people could achieve this destiny of being parents in total harmony with God. Instead of seeing the arrival of a glorious eighth day, the story in Genesis sadly tells us that something happened in the garden and that due to this situation God suddenly had to leave.

From now on, no matter what we are called to study horizontally in this world, even though it looks purely biological, chemical or mathematical, our studies should bring us to an awareness of the mechanics within the brain of God who created all things. As we become aware of the complexity of the creation, such as the sprouting of flowers, their processes of growth and eventual death, together with the vertical view that God is the Mastermind or Creator of those flowers, we will find ourselves unable to stop saying that these flowers and trees, rivers and mountains are really beautiful. Through this process we will surely fall in love with God or with someone who represents Him. With this recognition, God will become our first true love, our only love, and nothing will ever surpass that love or be able to melt our hearts more than He does.

Unless human beings choose this viewpoint, humanity will continue to be emotionally illiterate, and the citizens of our societies will continue to experience so-called psychological and emotional dilemmas on a daily basis. Indeed, because these problems are so pervasive in our civilization, it is easy to consider them normal, until the day when someone comes along with a serene heart, like Jesus must have had as he passed among the people of his time. It was for this reason that Jesus said to his disciples that unless you have peace within yourself you cannot have love, as he exclaimed in 1 John 4:20: "If anyone says, 'I love God', yet hates his brother, he is a liar. For anyone who does not love his brother, whom he has seen, cannot love God, whom he has not seen." In other words, as long as there is a war going on within us, love cannot exist.

Since the people who were around Jesus did not learn from him about how they could make peace within themselves by following the vertical line, Jesus had to depart from this Earth without leaving a strong legacy of love, besides some stories about his life. Due to that, no one after him could figure out how to remove the conflicts within themselves, and this is the reason that Paul said in Romans 7:23, "I see another law at work in the members of my body, waging war against the law of my mind and making me a prisoner of the law of sin at work within my members."

Jesus was not welcomed by the people around him and therefore he could not give his full knowledge. But worse than this, his dream of building the Kingdom on Earth was shattered, as he was. Therefore if today the focus of our education is similar to the education the people received at the time of Jesus, which was to memorize facts and create a pragmatic world where the law of survival was the main ingredient in building society, we can say that human beings of today appear to be similar to those living at the time of Jesus.

Surely this philosophy of education is perfect for making it impossible for love to be received or transmitted by human beings. Since everything exists in consideration of cause and effect, and internal and external realms, it is not surprising that people have so many mental and emotional problems. For example, if you choose to accept the view that the origin of life is only from matter, then the effect of that category of thought on your consciousness will be to think that you also are just a being of matter. And if you see the world as a place where knowledge is what creates your value, then you will believe you must acquire knowledge above anything else.

But regardless we are educated by methods of logic due to the way the secular world functions, we humans still hear a voice calling us from within to search for the deeper dimension within ourselves, just as children who were adopted by other parents still want to find their parents of origin. Due to this voice, some people try to search in the realm of origin for their first Parent, who is the invisible God.

There are other humans who follow another voice, which tells them that they are forbidden to look for their original, invisible Parent, and they choose instead to follow the viewpoint of a different parent, which is to focus on acquiring wealth and accumulating knowledge in order to gain power for themselves. But every so often someone will appear in the midst of the secular multitude, someone who is sounding a trumpet call, a cry for human beings to come back to the original Parent. Even though this person comes to them as a new prophet, human beings are usually so busy working for their other master that they do not have the strength to free themselves from their false parent who offers to them a world of illusion. But regardless of the focus of these people, they are still hoping and longing for someone to come from the original Parent, not just to speak to them, but to liberate them from bondage to the false parent.

Therefore we can say that if the chosen people and especially the women around him had responded to Jesus while he was alive and had learned the vertical viewpoint on how to perceive his Father through him, then God could surely have taken a rest from His constant worry. In that moment, for the first time God would have begun to experience happiness to see humanity arriving to the place where He had been waiting so long for them to arrive. Surely in this place they would no longer thirst for His love. Instead, this entire planet would be filled with the eternal water of life, where the river of God's love would flow inside the souls of all human beings, and this planet would no longer be called a lonely planet or a planet of despair.

If past history can be remade by us today, love will begin to accumulate within us, and we will find ourselves becoming softer and more moist and tender, while at the same time more firm and clear. As this love begins to compress inside us, we will become crystals of God's love. This is the reason Jesus said that he was the Rock, "And from this rock I will build my church" (Matt. 16:18), which means that Peter as the church had to unite with Jesus as the rock.

Today, if this lesson has created some interest to you, I hope it is not just to add some knowledge to what you already know, but will be a lesson of wisdom that will help you to see according to the way God hopes for you to see. If we can educate ourselves to be aware of everything as symbols of the love of God and to recognize God's love behind every person who gives something to us, at the very least we will become the kind of person that other people will want to be close to and stay with, not because of any laws or contracts but because of the elements of love within us.

If you have the dream to be in love with another individual being, check well if that individual is also in love with the One who is the Initiator of love before you give your life to that person. If you give your life to someone whose concept is that life is just fleeting and material, you will discover with time that this person is not able to become the substance of love. If you choose a person who is in love with the Origin of love, then you will know that this person has the ambition to take the same road as the one we call Jesus. If you find this person as your Christ, then surely you will feel secure and content as your days pass with him or her, because day by day your partner and you are becoming the image of God.

If I can give a word of wisdom to those of you who are still young and whose flesh does not yet exhibit wrinkles, remember that your flesh is only made for the purpose of protecting what you have not yet matured within it, which is a heart of love. The ideal is that by the time a person sees his or her skin starting to transform with age, this person's heart will be mature enough that love will be visible through his or her skin as it becomes thinner. Regardless you become old in years, your skin will shine with beauty and everyone will wish to come close to you. Therefore, if you do not want to waste money and time in keeping your skin in youthful condition, why not try the most natural way, which is to make yourself capable of receiving God's love?

Through this viewpoint we can say that regardless our lives begin as young people who look beautiful on the outside but are just beginning to put love inside their souls, one thing is sure, when we become old it is the love we carry within that will make us shining and ready to live in the other life, because we created ourselves as the image of God on Earth. Therefore, anyone from the younger generation will have no problem to believe that God is love or that God is real. When these young people see us as a mature person, they will wish to rest their heads upon our shoulders, hoping that one day they themselves can achieve the love they feel emanating from our flesh.

The view I am expressing here is very different from what we actually see people achieving in our world today. I think that I do not have to explain more about this to you. One thing is sure, what we have become is a sad story for God, which I hope, together, we can begin to erase, by each individual taking responsibility to create a new story for God. This new trajectory of each human being will be able to remove the regret God has had in creating human beings, as we find in Gen. 6:6, "The Lord was grieved that He had made man on the Earth, and His heart was filled with pain." Instead we should create new stories where we can be absolutely sure that God cannot resist turning His head toward us in hope of being close to us. The stories of our lives should make Him strain His ears to make sure He does not miss one little word we share with Him or with one another.

If Jesus is listening to what I say, I hope he feels free to go wherever you are and visit you, because in the moment you accept to see with both the vertical and horizontal viewpoint, I know that Jesus will come and begin to be your friend, your companion, and, why not, your first love? Then surely you can walk with him as your first love. As you pass through your lives, you will be fulfilling his dream for you, which is to become like him, and in the process you will find your own dream to be beautiful for the one who chooses to live with you being fulfilled as well.

For this reason I can say that Heaven and Earth will become one. And through that unity, all people will surely come to proclaim that there is a new Heaven and a new Earth.

I hope that you will take this road of the Christ, who calls each and every one of us to take the same path. If you accept to take this road of divinity, you will find yourself on the way to fulfilling the new Eden or the new Canaan. Then all the prophets who gave their hearts, souls and physical flesh to bring this road to the world will weep tears of great joy to see you, instead of crying from deep sorrow as Jesus did.

So if you feel this road inviting you, please take it with your flesh and soul until Jesus knows that you understand his heart.

Let it be so.

www.ingramcontent.com/pod-product-compliance
Lightning Source LLC
LaVergne TN
LVHW051544070426
835507LV00021B/2391